Women Under Glass

The Secret Nature of Glass Ceilings and the Steps to Overcome Them

Eric Shoars, Ph.D.

ISBN: 1-4392-6401-5
ISBN-13: 9781439264010

For Mom

Table of Contents

About the Author

Eric Shoars was bitten by the radio bug in elementary school. Since the age of six, when he received his first transistor radio as a Christmas gift, Eric's bedtime routine includes attempting to tune in AM radio stations from across the country. His love affair with radio and a high school job shadowing assignment launched Eric's on-air radio career at the age of 16. His career has covered three decades and has included being an on-air personality, assistant news director, sports play-by-play announcer, program manager, college educator, internet radio station operator, and certified branding consultant. He served on the board of directors of the Minnesota Broadcasters Association and has written articles for Radio World, Radio Ink, and Women's Business Minnesota magazines. WKRP in Cincinnati remains one of his all-time favorite television shows.

Eric has a Ph.D. in Organization and Management with a specialization in Leadership from Capella University in Minneapolis, Minnesota. He lectures, writes, and blogs on the subject of glass ceilings and is a continuing advocate for women in business. Eric's website is www.womenunderglass.com

Eric lives in Austin, Minnesota, with his wife Julie.

Praise for Women Under Glass

"In "Women Under Glass,"Eric Shoars clearly defines what keeps business women from the upper clout positions in most companies and the ramifications of doing so. Until leadership skills, expertise, and talent are evaluated without gender bias, businesses will neither truly reflect the culture of the consumer or the community, nor will they reap the benefits of seeing the world through balanced eyes."

Joan Gerberding, Principal, NextGenMarketing

"How interesting that this common sense manuscript was written by a man. What many women live day in and day out just might be a wakeup call for some of the opposite sex. At a time when many say we need to only look forward, through the meaningful and very practical comments remembered by the author of his mother coupled with quotes from other successful women, it proves we can not only learn a lot from the past but it may help all of us not only see through the glass ceiling but crack it and eliminate it."

Erica Farber, Former CEO/Publisher, *Radio & Records*

"Eric Shoars is to be commended for shedding light on a persistent problem. As one of the few women radio consultants, I have seen first-hand that the glass ceiling still exists; and as he points out, many highly qualified women continue to experience it. Eric has addressed a difficult subject in a style that is both insightful and informative. I hope his book generates some much-needed discussion.

Donna L. Halper, Author of *Invisible Stars: A Social History of Women in American Broadcasting*

Asst. Professor of Communication, Lesley University, Cambridge, Massachusetts

"This book provides an informative insight into the reasons that has allowed gender discrimination in the workplace to exist until now."
Nicki Gilmour, CEO of www.theglasshammer.com, the leading online community for professional women.

"Eric Shoars has given us what may be the definitive book on the subject.Women Under Glass is a game changer for women. For the first time we see glass ceilings as they really are and how they can be broken. This is a must-read for all women stymied by glass ceilings."
Marc Muchnick, Ph.D., Coauthor of *The Leadership Pill*

"Women have made enormous strides in the business world.That said, Eric Shoars argues compellingly that the progress should continue. I don't come to all the same conclusions that Shoars does but I certainly agree with the point that there are unlevel playing fields and they need a steam roller."
Kevin Hogan, Psy.D., Author of *The Science of Influence*

"Every woman in business should read this book.You will indeed break through the glass ceiling. Every male in business needs to read it too… to understand important issues, which if repaired in organizations will strengthen your business in many ways."
B. Eric Rhoads, CEO, Streamline Publishing, Inc.

"Eric Shoars challenges the assumption that glass ceilings are a problem of the past and uses a successful radio industry mentoring program as a blueprint to help women break through those upper limits. An academic essay that extends the metaphor and explores not just the existence but the construction of glass ceilings in an effort to take them apart … a feministic view of workplace obstacles, gender schemes, clout positions, and societal roles."
Paul McLane, U.S. Editor in Chief, Radio World

Foreword

By Kevin Hogan, Psy.D.
Author, *The Science of Influence*

The Glass Ceiling?

Eric Shoars argues in compelling fashion that there is a glass ceiling for women. Part of his thesis is that women have a difficult time securing positions of power in major corporations. Eric notes the wide gender gap at the boardroom table and in the CEO office. He quotes a statistic that shows that perhaps 4 times as many men have board/CEO positions compared to women.

Clearly there is a disparity in the gap between women on top and men on top.

On the other hand…

Women hold half the positions in the workforce in the United States. They get more college degrees than do men. Women's per capita income is stable where the income of men is falling dramatically, perhaps 10% adjusted for inflation, since 2000.

Women 65 and older are the only demographic to see a significant income increase in the first decade of the 2000s. (Up 20% since the millennium began.)

Counter this point of view with the fact that women earn 78 cents for each dollar a man is paid.

I was a Mr. Mom, a stay at home Dad for my daughter. I was the guy on duty for the first couple of years of her life. My wife was busy bringing home more money than I was so I was the logical appointee for daytime parenting.

My childhood, where a Father abandoned our family and my step-father died, caused me to take a leadership role in a family of six at the age of 8 and stay in that position for five years. There is no question that I get raising children as few men can. My respect for being the parent at home with the child is very high indeed.

However in those two years of being at home, I was not fine tuning my job skills so my wife jumped out in front of me in income to the tune of 20 or 25 percent when I returned to the workforce. I had essentially 'lost" a couple of years to the economy and couldn't command what she could upon my return simply because my experience was not as "great," certainly not as quantifiable.

I don't think that a corporation would discriminate against me by hiring my wife instead of me at that time (and perhaps not now!) because I was a stay at home Dad/A Dad. It's simple logic. Parenting is perhaps the most important skill we can possess next to providing a safe environment to parent in.
Had I stayed in the "corporate world" would I have not experienced a bias that she would have because she was female?

There's no way of knowing for sure.

Clearly when our next child came along, she lost her ground in the corporate world and my experience level (years in service) notched up.

My best guess is that biologically and culturally it is logical to predict that women would earn about 80% of what men earn if they both worked when able simply because of time lost and quantifiable experience levels simply not there.

All that said, certainly one can argue that the 1000 most talented or skilled business leaders in the United States are 80% male. Could THAT be true?

I find it hard to believe. That number should fall closer to 50/50 though probably not to 50/50 because there is a filtering process that takes place. A lot of very responsible parents will choose to have one parent work and one stay at home and raise children. This model is a good model and certainly no one should have to feel guilty because they are "'staying home with the kids." I promise you that is just as real as any other job. And no, I don't believe you should be "paid" for that "job" because it is not a job. It is work. There is a grand difference.

So back to our 1000 best and having only 10-20% of those leaders as women.

How does that happen?

Do women not pursue these positions?
Would some group of people hire an inferior man to run the show while a superior woman is standing in the wings?

That's a good question too. It's easy to say obviously the women aren't getting hired but when you break it down to a case by case basis, you would be foolish to not hire the best person for a job.

So does bias exist?

You bet. There is bias against women and men. There is bias against black and white. As long as there are differences and men and women are as different as night and day, there will be bias. Men and women process information differently in many ways. And the one factor that never changes is parenting. Women get pregnant, men don't. Talented, skilled women who would make great CEO's get pregnant, realize they love their children and tell Homer to go get a job because she wants to give and get as much out of being a Mother as she can.

You can't do anything but respect that.

My best guess is there are plenty of "Ole Boys Clubs." I've certainly seen them. Legal issues make them even more likely to stay cemented in our culture than ever before. In general men can speak to men in any tone with any word groupings and not be afraid of being sued or losing their job. The same words spoken to a woman could cost you and every male leader knows that. This doesn't stop promotion of females but it might at the highest levels. At some point women will force the issue and say, "We don't want the legal edge. We can handle anything you throw at us." For the same reason unions had value in the 40's but are destructive in the 00's, women's rights brought women to the MBA but may keep them out of the boardroom. Say the wrong words and pay for it? Easier to bring in Joe. Not as smart. No lawsuit going to happen there.

But is it that simple?

I don't know. I doubt it.

I suspect many, many factors play into the "why" and I obviously not only believe but am firmly in favor of the best players on the team playing. Period. For me, I want the profitable manager, the profitable CEO. It really doesn't matter who that person is. I know that in many places that isn't how it all plays out.

As you read this book, you'll see a compelling argument made for the glass ceiling and I think what Eric Shoars has done is brilliant in laying down the challenge to produce conversation and communication about an issue that shouldn't go away.

Kevin Hogan

1 WHAT MIGHT HAVE BEEN

Helen Shoars was born on December 14, 1927, and is a member of the acclaimed "Greatest Generation." Women in Mom's generation didn't have careers until World War II made working women a necessity. However, the women were sent back home to fulfill their traditional duties in the home once the men came home from fighting overseas.

In the 1950s and 1960s, women fought for social change and the opportunity to pursue their own destinies, particularly in the workplace. Mom was one of those women who sought to work outside the home in addition to being a housewife. Mom began her outside career as a Tupperware sales representative in 1959. Dad didn't like the idea of her working away from home but Mom convinced him to let her give it a try. Mom told Dad that if she didn't make sales manager within six months she'd give up selling for Tupperware. Dad agreed and a sales career was born. Mom achieved her goal, becoming a sales manager within six months. She recruited four women to work under her in a territory that covered Southern Minnesota and Northern Iowa.

Mom's next goal was to be a regional manager. A regional manager made more money and had more women working under her. Mom knew that regional manager was the highest she could go at Tupperware. She had a husband and six children who needed her and the time commitments necessary for Tupperware upper managers made it impossible to balance work and family.

In 1960 Mom was recruited to begin selling insurance. She traveled to Des Moines to take the state test to be licensed to sell insurance. Mom scored third highest out of the group of 90 and became a member of the first all-women insurance sales team in Iowa for American Mutual Life. It was during this time that Mom experienced situations over which she had no control.

In those days, the husbands usually bought the insurance and the wives went along with whatever the husband decided. Most men wanted appointments after work or in the evenings. The problem was that Mom was married and meeting a male client for supper or somewhere else at night was socially unacceptable. Even if Mom's boss wanted to take her to lunch, another woman from the sales team had to be included. Mom recognized that if she couldn't take male clients to supper she would be at a disadvantage to her male competitors trying to close deals. Dad also did not support her after-hours client meetings. Mom assessed the upside, the obstacles, and what she would need to do to advance her career. In the end, Mom decided there was only one option – she resigned from her insurance sales position.

Mom considered rejoining Tupperware but it was not to be. Mom and Dad were involved in a near-fatal car accident in Dexter, Minnesota, on March 11, 1961. Mom was in the hospital for almost a year and Dad for seven months. Both had to be taught to walk again. By the time she had fully recovered, the structure of Tupperware had changed. The managers and operations for Mom's territory were moved from Mason City, Iowa, to Washington state. Mom's career with Tupperware was over.

Mom and Dad bought a restaurant in Grafton, Iowa, in 1969 and opened for business on January 1, 1970. It truly was a family business, as a few of my siblings worked in the restaurant in full or part-time capacities. The five years Mom and Dad owned the restaurant were the only years I ever saw Mom work outside the home. They sold the restaurant in 1975, when I was seven. From that point on, any work Mom did was at home. She sewed professionally for many years, making everything from drapes to business suits. In the late '70s, Mom took painting lessons and opened a craft shop at home. Dad had a workshop where he made customized frames plus decorative items that Mom would paint and sell. The craft shop was a full-time business into their retirement years, until a fire destroyed it in 1994.

Mom would share stories about her sales career during the years she operated the craft shop. She spoke of her sales career fondly and I could tell it was a piece of her life that was unfulfilled. I wondered what would have happened if Mom had continued with her sales ambitions? How much would she have achieved? Where would her career success have taken her?

Mom is 82 now and she still talks with passion about selling. Mom says today she would sell anything that is profitable. If she were in better health, she'd be outselling people half her age. These days Mom offers painting, quilting, or sewing lessons to whoever wants to learn. Plus, Mom has written and is selling a series of children's stories. Mom excels to that which she puts her mind. She'll tell you she doesn't have any talent, she just works hard. Make no mistake, Mom will still outwork anyone in the room. Her drive, passion, commitment, resourcefulness, and tenacity make her someone who isn't satisfied with anything less than her best effort and result. She is the most amazing woman I've ever known. Still, I wonder what might have happened, had she continued her sales career? How far up the ladder could she have risen?

∽

I have been an on-air personality, assistant news director, sports play-by-play commentator, program manager, and certified branding consultant during 25 years in radio. In addition, I was the head of the Radio department at Riverland Community College, teaching the next generation of broadcasters and launching one of the first college internet radio stations in the state of Minnesota. I also served on the board of directors of the Minnesota Broadcasters Association.

In my 25 years in radio, I have personally noted, read articles in industry magazines, and heard stories from my network of industry peers regarding the lack of women in power positions in our industry. By "power positions," I refer to positions such as CEOs, COOs, CFOs, presidents, and vice-presidents. There are women in the radio industry attempting to achieve executive positions but are falling short, as most women in radio management are sales managers. That's where most women's ascension up radio's corporate ladder typically stalls.

Radio isn't the only industry where women are facing difficulties in achieving executive positions. In the early 1990s I became aware of the "glass ceiling." I took note of articles in national newspapers and magazines that focused on women in American business encountering this barrier. Story after story highlighted women who didn't accomplish their professional goals not because they weren't capable nor qualified but because they were women. Whether it was considered a societal "no-no" or blatant gender disqualification, women in business faced a barrier through which they were not allowed to pass. This "glass ceiling" bothered me and it raised a number of questions: Did such a barrier really exist? If so, what caused it? Was this barrier solely gender-based? Was this barrier a widespread phenomenon that all women faced or just a few? The glass ceiling phenomenon has been discussed and debated for the better part of 23 years and, yet, it seems women are not much better off now than they were then. Women are still struggling to achieve the power positions to which they aspire.

In September 2002 I began my doctoral studies at Capella University in Minneapolis, Minnesota. The radio industry and Mom crossed my mind when it came time to consider a dissertation research topic. I chose to explore and research glass ceilings. That research culminated in the discovery of the secret nature of glass ceilings, why they continue to be the powerful force they are, and how those glass ceilings can be broken. Now I'm going to share my discovery with you, so no one will have to ask "what might have been" anymore. Things have changed, but not as much as we'd like to think. There will still be, for a few more years, moms like mine who might have had different opportunities had glass ceilings, or the factors that create them, been nonexistent.

Feminist Sally Helgeson often quotes a Chinese proverb: "Women hold up half the sky" to remind us men and women not only have an equal stake but an equal responsibility in both skies of humanity – the private half (home and family) and the public half (business and jobs). Both halves must work together for the sky to be complete; nothing that excludes one half of humanity can be termed complete.

Traditionally, American society has assigned the home and family half of the sky to women, while the business and jobs half has been assigned to men. America's public sky continues to be dominated by men. If women are to hold up half of the public sky, they must have a presence, a voice, and active participation in the corporate boardrooms.

2 THE SKY IS LIMITED

The term *glass ceiling* was coined by the *Wall Street Journal* in 1986 to describe the barrier holding back businesswomen from the executive level of Corporate America. The term glass ceiling means different things to different people. For our purposes, glass ceilings are defined as *invisible barriers in the workplace that prevent women from attaining clout title positions.* Glass ceilings apply to women as a group, regardless the industry, who are kept from advancing to executive levels because they are women. Glass ceilings are a reflection that women are not being given access to the public half of the sky as it relates to clout title positions. This book will focus on how women fail to reach executive level positions – Chief Executive Officer, Chief Operating Officer, Chief Financial Officer, President, Vice-President, Board of Directors – otherwise known as *clout title* positions and how the glass ceilings they face can be overcome.

Glass ceilings have sparked discussion and debate as to their causes, effects, and possible solutions. However, the flaw with the debate and effort to break through glass ceilings is the focus on the effects of glass ceilings – i.e. few women in clout title positions and lower salaries for women compared to their male counterparts – rather than the exact cause(s). It is akin to treating a headache with an aspirin – and we're culturally trained to do that. We ease symptoms. But what's causing the headache? Tension? A brain tumor? High blood pressure? Misaligned vertebrae? Though glass ceilings are complex, they have some common causes, and we won't demolish glass ceilings until we address the causes. When discussing glass ceilings it is important to have a common understanding of what glass ceilings do in addition to what they are. There are several common threads in understanding glass ceilings:

• They pertain to women;
• They are invisible barriers preventing women from attaining clout title positions;
• They are a form of discrimination;
• They are created by attitudinal and organizational biases.

The most troublesome aspect of glass ceilings lies in their abstraction. Their invisibility makes them difficult to quantify. In attempting to see glass ceilings, we cannot measure them with a single, universal standard of measurement. What we can do, however, is examine some numbers to show us where glass ceilings begin.

Making the Invisible Barrier Visible

There are 82 men for every 100 board seats in America's boardrooms on the elite list of America's 100 companies. Women hold 12% of all S&P 500 corporate board seats. 15 Fortune 500 companies have female CEOs. Less than 10% of CEOs in either the Fortune 500 or Fortune 1000 are women. These figures show us glass ceilings have created and sustained barriers that keep women out of clout title positions. However, the more telling numbers are these:

• 40% of women financial executives perceive a glass ceiling, but only 10% of their male counterparts do.
• 66% of female financial executives said women face one or more obstacles to success in finance, but only 38% of male financial executives said women face such difficulties.
• 70% of female executives and 57% of male executives believe an invisible barrier – a glass ceiling – prevents women from getting ahead in business, according to a study of 1,200 executives in eight countries, including the United States, Australia, Austria, and the Philippines.
• 73% of male CEOs believe that the glass ceiling is no longer a problem for women, while 71% of women trying to break through glass ceilings said it is.

Talk about a difference in perspective! The continued power of glass ceilings is obvious when we compare the views of men and women in clout title positions. Men don't see or recognize glass ceilings; therefore, they don't exist. This difference in the perception of glass ceilings illuminates one of the critical components as to why glass ceilings still have the power to exclude: women are not being identified, recruited, and placed in executive management tracks, so they continue to be held back by forces they can't see and forces men *won't* see.

Men in clout title positions, who deny the existence of glass ceilings, are less likely to take aspiring women CEOs under their wings. These men may also believe there are not enough qualified women CEO candidates. Men in clout title positions won't recognize glass ceilings exist, in part, because advantaged groups actively attempt to preserve their advantage if subordinate groups are constantly attempting to take the dominant group's power. The advantaged group (men) in the business world can use glass ceilings to thwart the efforts by the subordinate group (women) to assume more clout title positions.

The difference in perspective also comes from how breaking through barriers is defined by society at large. Roger Bannister defied the conventional wisdom of his time and was a pioneer in the sport of running. However, just because he and others have broken the "four-minute barrier" doesn't mean that everyone can do it. So it is for women in business attempting to break through glass ceilings. Some women have done it so it is possible, but most women are far from being equal in opportunity to break through their barriers.

Women gained the right to vote in America in 1920. In 2007 – 87 years later – Nancy Pelosi became the first woman ever to be elected as Speaker of the House of Representatives. During her run for the White House in 2008, Hillary Clinton attempted something that had never happened: a woman being a major Party's nominee for President of the United States. These women, like the CEOs, CFOs, COOs, and Board of Directors in business, are the exception to the rule. Just because they broke through the barrier doesn't mean that barrier – the glass ceiling – has been broken for all women.

Following the suspension of Senator Clinton's presidential campaign, there was a discussion on the June 9th, 2008, edition of CBS TV's "Early Show" about whether Hillary Clinton had broken through a political glass ceiling. Political commentator Arianna Huffington told "Early Show's" Harry Smith that Senator Clinton's campaign was "more evolutionary than revolutionary." There are many areas in business and politics where women's achievement is evolutionary rather than revolutionary. Compensation achievement for women is also in an evolutionary stage.

In addition to fewer women holding clout title positions, women also find themselves being paid less than they're worth for doing the same type of work. Globally, women make 78 cents for every dollar earned by a man. However, the same percentage of men and women – 58% – felt they were fairly compensated. In the United States, 67% of men were happy with their salaries, compared with 60% of women. In 1979, women brought home only 68 cents for every dollar earned by a man. There is a brighter picture for women in Generation X and younger. By the year 2000, women 25-34 earned 82 cents for every dollar earned by a man on average. One of the factors in this generational increase is attributed to the fact that, in 1975, 18% of women ages 25-34 had completed four years of college. In 2000, 30% of women 25-34 completed a degree.

Beyond gender, one of the biggest challenges for women is to figure out what they're worth and stop taking less. For years, the disparity in pay was due to built-in biases but, in some cases, women are accepting less than they deserve. In the past twenty years, the focus of glass ceilings has been on the lack of women in clout title positions and the disparity in pay between men and women performing the same jobs. As noted earlier, these issues are not the cause of glass ceilings but are the result of glass ceilings.

The analogy of a headache was used to illustrate that the symptoms of glass ceilings are being addressed rather than what is causing them. We will understand the best way to break through glass ceilings and get women on a faster track to clout title positions once the actual cause(s) of glass ceilings are identified.

Stop the ride, I want to get off

There has been a trend developing over the past ten years: high-achieving women who are "opting out," quitting high-paying, sought-after jobs to raise children, care for aging parents, or just escape from the chaos that often accompanies dual-income couples. Family concerns can limit managerial aspirations, as there are women who choose to give up their careers for their family.

"She was doing what women often do: scaling back on work for the sake of family, with a clear-eyed realization that she was, simultaneously, torpedoing her chances for a climb up the ladder... It's a choice women often make with no particular social sanctions... But it's also the reason women may continue to be stalled at the lower rungs in organizations and men may continue to rule."
— *Lawrence Tischler*

Women who opt out do so because they want more balance in their lives or because the cost of rising to the top is too high. Women today are challenged, too, with being single mothers who have to balance both the public and private skies and have to make hard choices regarding which sky gets priority at a given moment. In 1975, 45% of women in the workforce had young children, compared to 70% by the year 2000. In 1975, 33% of young women with children younger than three were employed compared to 45% being employed in the year 2000.

"But when it's a painful choice between the client crisis and the birthday party, the long road trip and the middle schooler who needs attention,

the employee most likely to put company over family is the traditional,
work-oriented male...In other words, women may be happier not gunning
for power positions if it means they can work less and have a life."
  — Lawrence Tischler

Women today, whether they are married moms or single
mothers, face tough decisions when attempting to balance their
private and public skies. There are moments when the two skies
overlap and difficult choices must be made. Over time, there are
women who decide that the struggle of trying to balance the two
skies is too much if their families are negatively affected. Some
women decide to give up their managerial career goals and stay at
a lower, less demanding job that allows them to have more time
with their family. Citigroup's Sallie Krawcheck:

"People talk about having it all, and I want to tell them I don't. What
I have are two things that are very important to me: my children and my
career...I'm not very nice to my siblings. I don't see as much of my hus-
band as I'd like. There are many women who would not make the choices
I have made."

Some women decide to leave the business world entirely and
devote full-time attention to home and family. Melinda Wolfe,
Head of Professional Development at Bloomberg, says that the
women who do want to pursue a path to the top of Corporate
America should not be marginalized:

"Even if most women don't want to break the glass ceiling, the few
that do shouldn't be ignored. Sometimes their ambitions have been
tempered by a corporate culture that stifles their success. Sometimes they
choose circuitous career paths, taking some time to care for children, pre-
pare for career change, or work in the non-profit sector."

The women who choose to continue their journey up the
corporate ladder often do not take the same linear path that men

do. Women who take time off from their careers to have and raise children find themselves at a competitive disadvantage when they decide to resume their careers. During the time women are away from the workplace to have and raise children, their male counterparts continue on their journey uninterrupted. Women coming back after time away find their peers have passed them on the way up the corporate ladder. Women who choose a circuitous career path are often penalized for doing so.

Many workplaces impose limitations on deserving women who are disqualified from executive positions because they are women. Glass ceilings are more complex than gender alone, which is why women in Corporate America have not seen more rapid advances to clout title positions the past twenty years. A simple conversation opened my eyes to a new way of seeing glass ceilings and provided insight as to why glass ceilings are such a challenge.

ᘒ

December 18, 2003. Seth, Melanie, Cheryl, and I were driving to Minneapolis to see an NFL game between the Minnesota Vikings and the Kansas City Chiefs. My friend Seth also has an interest in leadership so I shared with him my research findings and theories during our drive to the game. Seth pondered and offered: "You're assuming that all glass ceilings are the same. I don't think they are. Think about ceilings in a house. Some ceilings are flat, some are vaulted, some are Cathedral style, and so on. Glass ceilings probably don't have a uniform shape either."

Seth stopped and allowed me to contemplate what he had just said. He had made an excellent point. My assumptions leaned toward a uniform glass ceiling for all women. What if that weren't the case? Seth continued, "Women in some industries or some organizations are hitting glass ceilings at different levels than women in other industries or organizations. Some women may think that glass ceilings aren't as much of a problem because they haven't hit their ceilings yet, because some industries' ceilings may be higher than other industries'. In a house you can see what shape and height plaster ceilings are. With glass ceilings, you can't."

Again there was silence as I let Seth's words sink in. I realized he was right.

Glass ceilings are a matter of perspective. Glass ceilings hold men up because the glass ceiling to men is really a floor. From a woman's perspective, glass ceilings hold them down because they are below it. What also holds women down is an incorrect assumption that glass ceilings are flat, or at least uniform in shape. Glass ceilings are much more complex. Looking at the various shapes, sizes, scopes, and heights of glass ceilings helps us understand why glass ceilings have remained the impediment to women they are.

I have uncovered forces – panes, if you will – which construct, reinforce, and deconstruct glass ceilings. There are six panes in constructing, reinforcing, and deconstructing glass ceilings – two panes for each aspect. Each of the panes interacts with each other in relation to whether they are constructing, reinforcing, or deconstructing glass ceilings.

Over the past 23 years, illustrations of glass ceilings in books and magazine articles have traditionally shown glass ceilings as being flat. As Seth pointed out to me, that's not the case with houses. If we take the ceiling metaphor to its logical conclusion, then we must accept that just as ceilings in houses can be flat, vaulted, or Cathedral in shape so too can glass ceilings in business have different shapes. This variation would explain why glass ceilings change from organization to organization and industry to industry. Some women think glass ceilings aren't as much of a problem because, in their industry, the ceiling is higher. Other women in different industries may hit their ceiling right away. The continuing challenge is that glass ceilings are invisible so it is difficult to be able to immediately recognize the shape of a particular glass ceiling in a particular business, or where the inevitable stopping point for women is from industry to industry.

Glass Ceilings Are Panes

Using the ceiling metaphor and accepting that glass ceilings assume different shapes, we need to accept that glass ceilings in Corporate America vary in:

- *height* (ten feet or twenty feet high),
- *shape* (flat or vaulted),
- *scope* (lower in one part of a house while higher in another) and,
- *construction* (single layer or multiple layers).

The *height* of glass ceilings is the point women encounter a barrier which prevents them from advancing into executive positions within organizations. The shape of glass ceilings is not identical from industry to industry or company to company. The *shape* of glass ceilings differs because some companies within the same industry view and promote women differently within their organization. The *scope* of glass ceilings illustrates that women encounter barriers at different levels from department to department across the organization. The *construction* reflects those forces that affect attitudes and organizational prejudices, which go beyond gender. The making of glass ceilings leads to exploring those variables that construct, reinforce, and deconstruct glass ceilings. The interaction of these variables can be seen in two ways: linearly and systemically. In a linear view, glass ceilings look like this:

Constructing		Reinforcing		Deconstructing		
Power positions	→	Organizational Culture	→	IGCI	←	Mentoring
Gender	→	Societal Roles	→	IGCI	←	Feminism

Figure 1 - Linear construction, reinforcement and deconstruction of glass ceilings

The panes in glass ceilings come in pairs. The first aspect in each column represents the internal forces (power positions, organizational culture, mentoring) while the second series of factors shown represents external forces (gender, societal roles, and feminism). The internal forces are how the public sky influences glass ceilings from inside the organization. The external forces are how the private sky influences glass ceilings from outside the organization.

Power positions, organizational culture, gender, and societal roles push down on women as glass ceilings are created and reinforced as the powerful men in the company and society express their view of women's competence in clout title positions. Mentoring is the internal force pushing back at glass ceilings as women try to demonstrate their competence to attain and achieve clout title positions. Feminism is the external force pushing back at glass ceilings as women attempt to persuade business and society that women are as capable as men to hold clout title positions.

In a systemic representation, glass ceilings look like this:

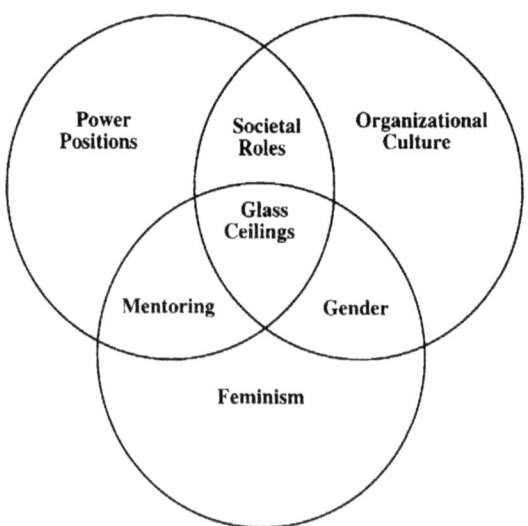

Figure 2 - Systemic representation of glass ceilings

The Venn diagram shows the intricate relationship each glass ceiling pane has to the others. The diagram resembles a kaleidoscope, which provides a lens through which to view glass ceilings.

Let me briefly explain the composition of each pane. These panes will be covered in greater detail in subsequent chapters.

Constructing panes

Power positions and gender construct glass ceilings. Power positions are those executive positions in the upper levels of businesses such as CEO, COO, CFO, president, vice-president, and the board of directors. If men in power positions do not believe women have the necessary aptitude for executive positions, women will not get promoted when a vacancy occurs. Gender in the business world reflects that the gender in power (men) has control over the destiny of the gender seeking power (women) and exercises it accordingly to keep the out-group (women) from becoming part of the in-group (men). Expectations of competence and what roles society views as proper for men and women are based solely upon the gender of the individual.

Reinforcing panes

Organizational culture and societal roles reinforce power positions and gender that construct glass ceilings. Organizational culture reflects the attitudes (spoken and unspoken, written and unwritten) of those in power positions and are passed down from generation to generation like an organizational heirloom. An organization's culture may mirror society's attitudes and assumptions. For example, societal roles say that women cook, men grill. Organizational culture makes similar assignments: men in the boardroom, women in middle management. Glass ceilings are strengthened as organizational culture reinforces power positions and societal roles reinforce gender assignments. However, there are two forces that counteract and deconstruct the constructing and reinforcing factors.

Deconstructing panes

Mentoring and feminism are the deconstructing panes of glass ceilings. Mentoring has been a recommended strategy to assist women past the invisible barriers. Mentors are able to sympathize

with the challenges women face on a daily basis and provide a
network of powerful people inside a company and/or industry.
These mentors can help change the perceptions of those in power
positions who make decisions regarding promotions and get more
women into clout title positions. Feminism has been characterized
as looking through the lens of gender – defined as sex as expressed
by social or culture distinctions – and seeing how it matters. In
part, feminists challenge our society to see how women in business matter, particularly in executive positions. Mentoring deconstructs power positions and organizational culture, while feminism
deconstructs gender and societal roles.

Until the perception of women's "shortcomings" changes among
those men currently occupying clout title positions, women's progress up corporate ladders will be slowed, if not stopped outright.

You're Not The Right Man For The Job

Women are perceived as lacking the characteristics executives
need to succeed and are judged to be less qualified leaders than
their male counterparts. This belief hinders women's ability to
break through glass ceilings. For example, there is a perception
that men compete harder than women. Women are viewed as un-
willing to do what it takes to win in the workplace and aren't seriously considered for executive promotions above certain levels.
Researchers Richard Martell and Christopher Parker noted that
women believe stereotypes and discrimination hold them back,
whereas men say it is women's lack of ability and desire.

One study showed women executives work as many hours a
week as male executives, but men compete harder than women,
were more willing to relocate, were more comfortable in putting
work ahead of personal commitments, were more likely to put
career ahead of family, and were less likely than women to experience work-life conflicts. The hard-driving image of the executive
is almost impossible for women to overcome in our culture, because women are still expected to hold up the private sky mentioned previously: home and family.

Mom experienced this in her sales endeavors because, even though she had a career, she was expected to first fulfill her duties as a wife and mother. Women often have to work harder than men because they are trying to hold up both halves of the sky at the same time. Even though the data contradicts the perception that women don't work as hard as men, it does not change the perception that men *compete* harder than women.

In addition, there is a clear double standard in how male and female executives are perceived and evaluated by the way they interact with their peers and subordinates. Columnist Rochelle Sharp:

"Male CEOs and senior vice-presidents got high marks from their bosses when they were forceful and assertive and lower scores if they were cooperative and empathic. The opposite was true for women. Female CEOs got downgraded for being assertive and got better scores when they were cooperative."

Most organizations still prefer to find senior executives from within their own ranks, perpetuating the old boy network in which a limited range of job titles and experiences artificially restricts the candidate pool. Old-boy networks not only reinforce the male-friendly values and attitudes but also lead to gender bias in key decisions. Men's expectations of women's competence – or incompetence – determine the opportunity for women to achieve clout title positions, regardless of the actual competence of the women.

Traditional prerequisites and qualifications for senior management and board of director positions focus too narrowly on conventional sources and experiences such as:
- Men being perceived as more aggressive than women;
- Men being perceived as risk takers;
- Men being groomed for promotion by those in clout title positions;
- Men having an uninterrupted track record of accomplishments.

The challenge for women in achieving executive positions involves overcoming stereotypes and schemas held by those in clout title positions. If it's a matter of actual qualifications, qualities, or perceived roles, women must change how those in clout title positions perceive women as leaders above middle management.

Gender schemas

In our culture, shared gender schemas are the "DNA" of the gender system, since they form the cultural rules with which people perceive and enact gender differences and inequality. This "genetic code" is in all of us from birth. Primary and secondary sex characteristics are truly what's carried in our genetic code – but how people *react* to those differences also seems encoded since birth. Society instills in us from day one what is and is not proper for each gender.

As our lives continue, society consistently shows us what is proper for boys and girls, from childhood to adolescence to adulthood. We generally react and respond according to what society has taught us. Evidence indicates that gender schemas contain beliefs associating greater overall competence with men than women, particularly in more valued social arenas, while also granting each sex particular skills, such as mechanical ability for men and domestic skills for women. These societal attitudes toward gender in the workplace are expressed to disqualify women from clout title positions. Women are kept from America's boardrooms based upon expectations or assumptions, not an actual track record.

The distinction between stereotypes and schemas is crucial and provides another key insight as to why women have not had more success breaking through glass ceilings. Stereotypes are hypotheses regarding how we expect others to act, either individually or as a group. "White men can't jump" or "Asians are good at math" are a couple examples of stereotypes. Stereotypes relate to the external glass ceiling factors of gender (constructing), societal roles (reinforcing), and feminism (deconstructing). External influences upon glass ceilings play a part as to what roles in our society are seen as acceptable for women.

"The essence of "comfort" lies in a woman's ability to defy expectations, even as the factors that make that so difficult are themselves the product of the differing expectations of men and women. Women make men comfortable by proving that they are not like other women, thereby affirming the very stereotypes of women that become, for most, self-fulfilling prophecies. Because it is expected that women will do less well, they must do better."
— Susan Estrich.

Virginia Valien says schemas, as opposed to stereotypes, affect our *expectations* of men and women, our evaluations of their work, and their performance as professionals. Schemas are an internal influence upon glass ceilings related to the expectations of women and the differences in perception as to their competency and effectiveness in the workplace. Schemas relate to the internal glass ceiling factors of power positions (constructing), organizational culture (reinforcing), and mentoring (deconstructing). Internal influences on glass ceilings play a part as to how women's effectiveness is perceived and evaluated by those who determine who does and who does not get promoted.

All schemas influence how we perceive and treat group members. When gender schemas are applied, qualities that emphasize a man's gender results in a small advantage, a plus mark; whatever emphasizes a woman's gender results in a small loss for her, a minus mark. Gender schemas contain status beliefs that associate greater status worthiness and competence with men than with women. Women can be dismissed as being "too emotional" or "not being tough enough to be a manager," or people think "a woman's place is in the home".

Specific status beliefs related to gender shape men's and women's assertiveness, the attention and evaluation their performances receive, any ability attributed to them on the basis of performance, the influence they achieve, and the likelihood that they emerge as leaders. Gender schemas have placed women in a precarious position as they attempt to get promoted from middle management to clout title positions:

"Women are, in most situations, expected to assimilate into the male-oriented culture by learning to act like guys. Alternative roles aren't any better. Geishas get jobs because they've got great legs, dress well, or in some way decorate the boss' office. They endure routine flattery – 'you're such a treasure!' – and in the process, they end up trivialized. Assertive women get labeled as bitches. There's even a program in California for 'bully broads,' women whose assertiveness scares men and whose companies send them off to finishing school to learn how to temper their 'challenging' behavior."
– *Margaret Heffernan*

The three management archetypes women in middle management can choose from – geisha, bitch, or guy – are examples of women behaving how they believe they must to advance up the corporate ladder. The behavior most men in power positions want women to exhibit is what women are instructed at an early age to do – act like a lady, don't make waves, and try and get along.

Gender status beliefs also create legitimacy reactions that penalize assertive women leaders for violating the expected status order and reduce their ability to gain conformity with directives. If a male leader's directives are followed without question by some individuals, then other members of the organization will more than likely follow suit. They see his leadership as legitimate. However, if a female leader's directives are sneered at or blatantly disregarded, then other members of the organization will see her leadership as illegitimate. Therefore, women will be seen and perceived as weaker, less effective leaders and thus not destined for clout title positions. Compounding matters, a study showed that female managers are more than three times as likely as their male counterparts to underrate their bosses' opinions of their performance. This discrepancy in performance perception increased with women older than 50.

As women begin to understand and actualize their strengths and goals, they gain a sense of purpose and an awareness of their collective identity as businesswomen. Virginia Valien believes that there are a number of potential pitfalls for women professionals, which originate with gender beliefs:

"Women must appear neither too feminine nor too masculine. At either extreme they make others uncomfortable. A woman who is very feminine runs the risk of seeming less competent; the more she typifies the schema for a woman, the less she matches the schema for a successful professional. On the other hand, a woman with more masculine traits runs the risk of appearing unnatural and deviant. The more she typifies the schema for the successful professional, the less she matches the schema for a woman."

In short: women are damned if they do and damned if they don't. The schema dynamic is an issue in:
- how men and women are evaluated,
- who is in line to be promoted,
- who gets promoted,
- how many men get promoted versus how many women get promoted.

Women aspiring to clout title positions are told they can't act like a woman and shouldn't act like a man. However, women still won't be promoted because they're not like the men who have the power to promote them. More men will be in the promotion pipeline. The answer for women seeking to break through glass ceilings is not to get more women in the pipeline for promotion but to diagnose the root causes of glass ceilings and use commensurate means to eliminate those ceilings. President of the Center for Worklife Policy Sylvia Ann Hewlett:

"The old idea was, all you needed to do was fill the pipeline with women and wait around for a couple of decades for them to move through the ranks. [But] there's an enormous amount of leakage from the pipeline — once women off-ramp even for a short while, it's incredibly difficult to get back in."

The radio industry is an example of how the pipeline theory fails to move women through the ranks. An overwhelming majority of those individuals currently holding executive positions in radio are men. For years women have been told much of the problem is that women need to get into the executive pipeline so that there are experienced radio women to choose from when executive positions come open. The "pipeline" seems to be a "pipe-dream". According to the April 2009 MIW (Mentoring and Inspiring Women) Gender Analysis, female radio station general managers have risen from 11.1% in 1995 to 15.8% in 2008, while female program directors have risen from 8.2% in 1995 to 10.9% in 2008. Mentoring and Inspiring Women member Joan Gerberding:

> *"If station managers had this little amount of growth in their revenues over a ten-year period, they would not keep their jobs. Yet we accept it in areas of diversity growth. Now on the bright side, since 1995, there has been a 21% increase in female general sales managers. In fact, women account for nearly one-third of all general sales managers of all radio stations in the country. Clearly we (women) can bring the money in."*

Simply getting more women in the pipeline is not enough to ensure that more women will achieve clout title positions or even be in the candidate pool for those positions. In the bottomline corporate world we live in, many executives are judged upon their ability to increase profitability, revenue, and value for their owner-ship group(s) and shareholders. These executives must not only show value to the company but *create* value for the company. What matters most for women who aspire to clout title positions is not to be judged by their gender but to be judged by their ability to show and create value for their organization.

Many terms have been used in attempting to make glass ceil-ings visible: internal and external influences, power positions, gender, organizational culture, societal roles, mentoring, and femi-nism. All of these aspects show us that glass ceilings are complex and cannot be overcome by focusing on a singular aspect. It is important for us to understand how each pane of the glass ceil-ing system works and how altering one pane affects all parts of the system. To that end, I will use a mythical company to illustrate each pane of the glass ceiling system, how each pane affects women's ability to achieve clout title positions, how each pane of the system relates to other panes, and, ultimately, how to create a new system that allows women to break through glass ceilings in Corporate America.

Our mythical company is Big Deal Foods. Big Deal Foods is a food processing and packing company founded in 1962 by CEO emeritus Harper Jones. Originally a small town enterprise, Harper Jones built his small company into a national corporation with meat processing and packing plants across the United States. In 1982 Big Deal Foods became a publicly traded company on Wall Street. Mr. Jones is "old school" and believes that women should work in the home raising families. He claims women do not have the toughness to survive in ruthless corporate boardrooms. We'll use Big Deal Foods to illustrate how glass ceilings are constructed and reinforced.

"In the 1920s and 1930s jobs for women were few. Women executives, if there were any, were few and far between. Women were limited to 'domestics', teachers, hair dressers, and bank employees. Glass ceilings were unheard of; our obstacle course was called 'climbing the ladder'."

– Helen Shoars

3 BRING ON THE GLASS CEILING

Harper Jones graduated with an MBA and a dream: to start his own company and turn it from a local enterprise to a Fortune 500 company. Harper's father worked for thirty years as a meat packer at a local meat processing and packing company. Harper himself had worked at the same company each summer as he put himself through college. Harper found he enjoyed the business and decided that one day he would start his own meat processing and packing company. After graduating from college, Harper Jones was hired full-time at the meat processing and packing company. Through the years, Harper learned more about the business and rose through the ranks until he became General Manager. In 1962, at the age of 42, Harper Jones founded Big Deal Foods.

Harper Jones' parents had a traditional marriage: Harper's father provided for the family while Harper's mother worked at home and took care of the family. Harper's marriage was the same. He was the father of five children – three sons and two daughters – and he encouraged his sons to be captains of industry and his daughters to find a husband and raise families. Harper believed a woman's place was in the home. Leave business to the men, he thought.

Over the years, Harper begrudgingly accepted that the workplace was not exclusively a man's domain and allowed women to be hired at Big Deal Foods. However, women were only to be hired as receptionists, secretaries, and salespeople. Harper believed that women did not possess the leadership qualities necessary nor have what it took to make the tough decisions needed in Corporate America.

When Harper Jones put together his first set of executives in place at Big Deal Foods, all those executives were men. Harper made no secret of his disdain for women in business and his belief

that men were best equipped for leadership. In the 20 years
Harper ran the company, no woman was ever hired or promoted
to a clout title position. Some brave managers broke with tradition and hired women as mid-level managers, particularly in sales.
None of the executives at Big Deal Foods was ever brave enough
to promote or hire a woman to a clout title position because no
one wanted to contradict Harper's philosophy. After all, they had
their own careers to think about. Through those years, all of his
managers, (including his son Colin) held firm to the practice that
no women were to be promoted above a mid-level management
position.

In 1982, as his last act as CEO, Harper Jones took Big Deal
Foods public. In the first act of the new board of directors, many
hand-picked by Harper himself, Colin Jones was elected as the
new CEO of Big Deal Foods. Harper, now retired, would retain a
title and have input on company policy, but have no official say or
vote on the board. Twenty-five years later, Harper's influence was
still evident. No women had been hired or promoted to a clout
title position at Big Deal Foods. The unwritten policy that Harper
created and enforced is still the rule at Big Deal Foods.

Historically, people have assumed that glass ceilings were a product of men versus women in an attempt to keep women out of the
man's domain. There is some truth to that sentiment. But if we
look at that dynamic as the only thing that creates glass ceilings,
we're missing some ways to understand how glass ceilings are
really constructed.

We know that glass ceilings are invisible, artificial barriers that
bar women from top executive jobs. Glass ceilings are a product
of attitudes and organizational prejudices that lead to occupational
segregation. Glass ceilings prevent women from achieving or
competing on a level playing field with men. However, these com-

monly held ideas do not reflect how glass ceilings are made, nor the multi-faceted nature of this creation.

Women who aspire to clout title positions feel the impact glass ceilings have on their careers, but they can't see how to get through those glass ceilings – because they can't see the attitudes that created the ceiling. My research revealed that power positions and gender actually construct glass ceilings. These constructing panes of glass ceilings, as well as the panes' invisibility, provide significant challenges for women to adequately assess the obstacles they're up against.

Power positions

Power positions, those positions characterized as clout title positions, are executive positions in the corporate world that have traditionally been held and dominated by men. These positions include CEO, COO, CFO, president, vice-president, and/or any other high-powered position in a company or corporation. Women's under-representation in clout title positions can be explained, in part, by messages they are given about the promotion process and the requirements of senior jobs. Men traditionally have risen through the corporate ranks because another man in a clout title position saw potential in the junior male employee and took "the ambitious young buck" under his wing. Women do not rise through the corporate ranks because men who do the promoting use their schemas to form expectations of men and women, evaluations of their work, and their performance as professionals. The expectations of women are lower, as is the perceived worth of women in the boardroom. These expectations and perceptions in companies are never verbalized, and they feed the invisibility of glass ceilings.

Men in power have traditionally opted to hire or promote those individuals who look and act like them – men. Men in clout title positions may believe women do not belong in or have the competence for executive positions. Power positions are an internal force that influences glass ceilings because members inside the company affect promotions to those positions.

In the case of Big Deal Foods, Harper Jones believed women were meant to stay at home and raise families and not to be captains of industry. Even though women were eventually hired, they were not promoted above mid-level management so Big Deal Foods set the ceiling for women at mid-level positions. The male executives' belief about women's incompetence was based solely on the fact that they're women: nothing more. No woman had been allowed to prove anything else. To be blunt, breasts were an immediate disqualifier for clout title positions.

Gender

Gender has been characterized as more than a trait of individuals. Gender is an institutionalized system of social practices establishing males and females as different in socially significant ways and organizing inequality in terms of those differences. We base our first assumptions and expectations of people on their gender before any other trait. Then we decide whether to elevate or diminish their level of equality based upon the context of what society has taught us is proper for that gender. We make this perception in some cases before we even meet the individual. We "know" everything we need to know about a person simply because of his or her gender.

Society assigns symbols to represent the "correct" gendered behavior or appropriate gender object. For example, when a baby boy is born, our society designates the color blue as a "boy color" whereas when a baby girl is born, our society designates the color pink as a "girl color". Traditionally, baby boys are dressed in blue and have blue-colored bedrooms. Baby girls are dressed in pink and have pink-colored bedrooms.

As adults, cooking in the kitchen is considered to be a woman's job, whereas barbequing outdoors is considered to be a man's job. It's culturally acceptable for a girl/woman to show emotion (especially crying), but "big boys don't cry." Society assigns gender to cars (often referred to with the feminine pronoun "she"), countries ("Mother Russia," the "Fatherland" of Germany), and employment (nursing and teaching are women's jobs; medicine and construction are men's jobs).

If we see a male construction worker, we see that as normal because men are "big and strong" and do tough work. If we see a female construction worker, we may see her as doing "unbecoming" work, or as marginally capable in her job, since women tend not to be as physically strong as men. Construction jobs are seen by society as being an appropriate occupation for men based solely upon physical characteristics. Even if a female construction worker did her job as well as her male colleague, she wouldn't be perceived to have the same competency as a man because we have no gender schema for female construction workers.

These attitudes toward gender in the workplace are expressed to disqualify women from clout title positions. Therefore, our expectations for the women are lower and women are paid less since they are perceived as not being able to do the same level of work or having the same level of competence as their male co-workers. Our twin headache issues regarding the lack of women in "male jobs" and lower pay than men is in full effect. The glass ceiling is firmly in place.

Glass ceilings are more complex than simply "men versus women," even though most of this chapter has highlighted how men are keeping women out of clout title positions. What has been illustrated is how men in power positions have put these glass ceilings in place. We now know what glass ceilings are, what they do, and how they're constructed. Thanks to help from Big Deal Foods, our glass ceiling is in place. In the next chapter it will be shown how glass ceilings are reinforced by organizational culture and societal roles.

"I was brought up in a family where I was taught that
I had the ability to do anything I set my mind to do.
If the ladder was kicked out from under a person,
simply get up, set the ladder up, and start again."
  – Helen Shoars

Reflections Under Glass

Reflections Under Glass is a collection of quotes from women in various industries who are battling glass ceilings in their field of endeavor. Their thoughts provide additional context to glass ceilings in Corporate America. The focus of Reflection Under Glass in each chapter will be on the specific glass ceiling panes spotlighted.

"I have to prove myself a few more times than a guy would have to prove himself, because women succeeding in a man's world is fairly new territory — especially for race-car driving. In this sport, the rules are the same for women and men. This shows that women can compete with men under the same guidelines."
Danica Patrick, Formula One race car driver

"Yes, there is a glass ceiling for women. But when I started to work, it was the laundry room. Today, it's the great room — the one with twenty-four foot ceilings — so we've come a long way."
Roberta Puschel, managing director at J.P. Morgan and former vice president of New York's Federal Reserve Bank

"My theory is that men apply for jobs two years before they're ready and women apply two years later than they ought to. Men don't allow their lack of experience to get in the way, whereas women must feel that they are entirely prepared for a job and that they've ticked all the boxes."
Lorraine Heggessey, CEO "talkbalkTHAMES"

Glass Ceiling Construction Terminology

Clout title positions – those positions that wield the most corporate influence and policy making power (also known as power positions). The term *clout title positions* was coined by Catalyst, a non-profit research and advisory organization working to advance women in business.

External influences – those factors such as gender, societal roles, and feminism that affect glass ceilings from outside companies or corporations.

Gender – sex as expressed by social or culture distinctions. Gender can refer to types, or kinds, of behavior that are associated by some order of social convention with a particular sex.

Glass ceilings – invisible barriers in the workplace that prevent women from attaining clout title positions.

Internal influences – those factors such as power positions, organizational culture, and mentoring that affect glass ceilings from inside companies or corporations.

Schemas – our expectations of men and women, our evaluations of their work, and their performance as professionals. Schemas are an internal influence upon glass ceilings related to those expectations.

Stereotypes – our hypotheses regarding how we expect others to act, either individually or as a group. Stereotypes are an external influence upon glass ceilings as what roles in our society are seen as acceptable for women and men.

4 CALL FOR REINFORCEMENTS

The story of glass ceilings is far from complete once power positions and gender have constructed the initial barriers. Once glass ceilings are created, they are reinforced by two additional panes – organizational culture and societal roles. Power positions are reinforced by organizational culture and gender is reinforced by societal roles. Gender and societal roles foster our gendered "genetic code". A further exploration of societal roles comes later in this chapter. First it is necessary to examine how those in power positions establish and sustain an organizational culture that perpetuates men's dominance in the boardroom.

What Is Organizational Culture?

When we speak of an organization's *culture* we are referring to the dominant attitudes, assumptions, and actions that represent the core values shared by most of the organization's members. Organizational culture provides a set of core characteristics that are collectively valued by the members of the organization. *Shared values* refer to appropriate actions and standards of conduct by members of the organization as judged by those members. Organizational culture is an internal factor that reinforces glass ceilings. There are three key functions of organizational culture.

Organizational culture:
- Provides a sense of identity for its members. The more clearly an organization's shared perceptions and values are defined, the more strongly people can associate themselves with their organization's mission, goals, and objectives and feel they are part of it;
- Provides a commitment to the organization's mission. People struggle with thinking beyond their own needs,

interests, and desires. A strong, overarching culture reminds people of what the organization is about;

* Provides a clarification and reinforcement of standards of
  behavior.

Organizational culture guides the employees' words and
deeds, making it clear what should be done or said in a given
situation, providing stability to behavior. An organization's belief
system, along with the translation and enactment of beliefs by its
leaders, will have a clear effect on the way things are done, how
the organization is experienced by its members, and the resulting
development of an organizational culture.

The core values are intensely held and widely shared within
the organization. Some organizations have very strong cultures.
Strong cultures have a greater influence on the behavior of its
members. Traditionally, women's success in the business world
– as defined by salary and promotion – depends on the learning
and coping behaviors in a hierarchical workplace defined by men,
who perceive the world as a competitive one, in which people are
either one-up or one-down. This view of business is described as a
zero sum game.

I win, you lose

Zero sum describes a situation in which a participant only gains
at the expense of another participant – or when a loss by any
participant benefits another participant. In order for someone to
win, someone else must lose. The context of the zero sum game
in the workplace comes down to a man's worldview of competi-
tion versus a woman's worldview of cooperation. Rules govern
the workplace and, historically, men have written those rules.
Knowing the rules of the game – and knowing whose rules they
are is a critical component to career success.

Gail Evans says that if business is indeed a game then, like
any game, there are rules to playing well. Men typically know

these rules because they wrote them. Women are at a disadvantage in the workplace because they don't know nor fully understand the rules of the game. Women often feel shut out of the process because they don't know when to speak up, when to ask for responsibility, what to say at an interview, and other key moves that can make or break a career. Women are forced to guess, improvise, and bluff when it comes to playing the game in the workplace because they don't have a copy of the "directions manual" of the organization and therefore aren't always sure how to proceed in climbing the corporate ladder. Evans states that men have always had the "directions manual" for work:

"And what about men? They don't read direction manuals, you say. True. They don't need to. The male mind invented the concept of directions. It wasn't that they deliberately ignored women, or disliked what women had to say. Rather, as business culture developed few women were around to help. Men wrote all the rules because they wrote alone."

Evans' comments underscore that there may not be a conspiracy to keep women out of clout title positions, but something does exist that has the same effect. Career survival can come down to being able to understand the context of the workplace and adjust accordingly.

The identity, commitment, and standards of behavior produced by organizational culture are established through a series of written guidelines that clearly define what is required from members. Written rules are all the formal, official, and understood aspects of the business. These written rules include vision statements, organizational charts, and policies. However, unwritten rules often carry more weight in the attitudes and behavior of people in the workplace than written rules.

Unwritten Rules

Unwritten rules are an extension of written rules and, ultimately, organizational culture. You do not need to have explicitly formulated rules to know the rules and how to act upon them. If one co-worker says to another, "That's not the way we do things here," he or she is expressing an unwritten rule of the organization. The unwritten rules according to researcher Peter Scott-Morgan:

- Give shape, context, and meaning to an organization's written rules;
- Are formal and informal in nature and shape how people within organizations behave and expect new members to behave;
- Are not always known by organization members since those rules are not codified in an employee handbook or other such documents;
- Start with top management and correspond to the internal politics of a business;
- Are manipulated by successful employees to their advantage;
- Are the missing links in our understanding.

The unwritten rules are treated as the official rules of the organization because savvy people "decode" a hidden meaning of the written rule and manipulate the rules to their personal benefit. Uncovering the unwritten rules will help the people understand the hidden sources of success in another part of the business. Here are some examples from Peter Scott-Morgan of written rules and the unwritten rules that are communicated to members of the organization:

Written rule: "To become a top manager, you need broad experience."

Unwritten rule: "To get to the top, job-hop as fast as possible."

Written rule: "Managers are accountable for their profit and loss."

Unwritten rules: "Protect your own turf" and "Watch your quarterlies".

As unwritten rules relate to glass ceilings, there may not be a formulated policy but it could be understood that women don't get promoted beyond a certain level. This unwritten rule could be expressed in organizations by the belief that "women aren't management material." The difficulty in changing unwritten rules – and the attitudes behind them – lies in the fact that men find it harder to go against social norms that are meant to favor them. It is natural for an advantaged group (men) to try to keep the advantage it enjoys. This dynamic makes it more difficult for the disadvantaged group (women) to persuade members of the advantaged group to assist them in changing social norms within organizations.

Men in power positions set the minimum standards to be met by employees, creating a culture that supports those standards. Those promising executives who look, act, and work like those in power are at a distinct advantage over those who do not. People struggle with thinking beyond their own needs, interests, and desires. A strong, overarching culture reminds people of what the organization is about. Consequently, the dominant group may not be willing to extend opportunities to unproven people – women. These social norms result from the learned societal roles that communicate some roles are men's roles while other roles are reserved for women.

Societal Roles
Societal roles are a reinforcing pane to gender in glass ceilings. Societal roles:
- Tell us how each gender should act and what activities are acceptable for each;
- Are an external reinforcing factor in glass ceilings;
- Are passed down from generation to generation as a sort of "cultural heirloom";

- Are a learned response to how adults teach children proper behavior for men and women;
- Are taught to children from the day they're born and continue throughout life.

Since adults endorse these gender norms, children perceive it as implied approval that certain actions, beliefs, and attitudes are not only correct but *the proper thing*. This socialization and process orientation is seen in how children structure and organize their play; the play behaviors translate into the workplace later in life. Sally Helgeson describes socialization this way:

"Male children learn to put winning ahead of personal relationships or growth; to feel comfortable with rules, boundaries, and procedures; and a submerged individuality for the greater goal of the game. Females learn to value cooperation and relationships; to disdain complex rules and authoritarian structures; and to disregard abstract notions like the quest for victory if they threaten harmony in the group as a whole."

For male-male interaction, relationships are secondary to reaching the goal, but preserving relationships is a central component in the female culture. The intra-gender social structures boys and girls learn as children come into conflict for men and women in the workplace, where social structures are inter-gender.

Helgeson also believes that in the current business culture, men continue to perceive business as they do sports – a hierarchical game with goals. Women see business as a web of relationships that move forward in a continuous process. Relationships with co-workers are tools men use to get the job done, while women see relationships as a key part of the business world, just as in their personal lives. Competitiveness, a trait generally ascribed to men, tends to inspire what people perceive as necessary qualities of leaders. Necessary qualities attributed to leaders include "aggressive," "tough-skinned," and "tough-minded." These traits of leaders are usually applied to men.

Decision-makers occupying clout title positions in organizations value the above qualities assigned to men and make decisions regarding promotions for that reason. This also explains why men continue to occupy a majority of clout title positions. These leadership qualities typically assigned to men (and the schemas that influence perception of people throughout organizations) underlie what is seen as the norm. People in clout title positions are more likely to hire people who are like them and hold similar values. Men view relationships in business as a means to an end in achieving professional goals. They form relationships with other people who can advance their careers. If an individual is part of the "in crowd," then they tend not to form relationships with the "out crowd."

Relationships tend to be closed when organizational members believe they can improve their situation through monopolistic measures. Those monopolistic measures are expressed through the perception of socially acceptable roles for men and women. Individuals who observe and support those roles are ones that will be looked upon with favor, while those who go against tradition will be looked upon with disfavor and treated accordingly. This effect is also known as *social closure*. Our society embraces women fulfilling their roles of childbearing and childrearing, but doesn't always embrace some women's desires to also be captains of industry, traditionally the men's domain. Those women who try to fulfill more than one role can find their lack of professional support a formidable obstacle in the workplace.

Men and women alike can satisfy many roles – personal and professional. Some of the roles women attempt to achieve may be frowned upon. A woman attempting to achieve a clout title position, while also being a wife and mother, faces difficult decisions. She must decide who or what has priority at a given moment and then face poor evaluation by those in clout title positions who may disagree with her priorities. If men in power positions believe women in their organization are giving too much weight to family or children's issues, those women could be disqualified from future promotions.

"She was doing what women often do: scaling back on work for the sake of family, with a clear-eyed realization that she was, simultaneously, torpedoing her chances to climb up the ladder...It's a choice women often make with no particular social sanctions...But it's also the reason women may continue to be stalled at the lower rungs in organizations and men may continue to rule."
– Lawrence Tischler.

Working mothers who are facing daily challenges in balancing work and family make sure, as best they can, that neither their personal nor professional obligations get shortchanged. Men may complain in the office about how overworked they are and how it affects them, but they rarely fight the "balance battle". Working mothers arise early each morning getting their children ready for school even as they get ready for work and feel lucky if they don't have spit up on their suits as they dash for the office. Working mothers, through their daily balancing act, may gain critical skills and insight that are of value in business.

An article by Anita Bruzzese in the May 2, 2005, *Des Moines Register* quoted a study which claimed skills such as consensus-building, recognition and reward, negotiation, planning, organization, collaboration, and helping others reach their potential are all part of a mother's daily job. These skills are also necessary in the office, particularly by those in clout title positions. Men in power positions overlook these traits in women choosing instead to judge their perceived commitment to the company. If women choose to balance work and family, men in power positions assume those women are not willing to make the commitment deemed necessary to be a successful executive. This is especially true if women take time off from their career in favor of spending time with young children or aged parents.

Women taking "non-linear" career paths find it difficult to build "on ramps" back to work after their career pauses. It can be done, however. Women such as Meredith Viera, who left a high profile job at CBS' "60 Minutes" program to spend time with her children came back to television on ABC's "The View" and is now co-host of NBC's "Today" show. Brenda Barnes, who left a top job with PepsiCo in 1998 to spend more time with her children, became the CEO at Sara Lee in 2006. The issue of on-ramping is not a new one. For years women have been trying to find the best way to balance family responsibilities with a high-stress career. A survey of midcareer women who hold college degrees found 37% had taken extended breaks from work, with an average off-ramper staying home for 2.2 years. Most of these women wanted to return to work, but just 40% regained full-time employment. Some businesses such as Marathon Oil, Federal Signal, and Booz Allen Hamilton have instituted programs to assist women back to the on ramp.

Despite the focus on helping female professionals to on-ramp, there's concern that women who make it back on track will still suffer from the larger problems facing female professionals, such as lack of high-ranking role models and lack of access to informal networks. High-ranking role models and informal networks are two aspects of deconstructing glass ceilings – mentoring and feminism – that are keys to women in breaking through glass ceilings. Mentoring and feminism will be examined in the next chapter.

Big Deal Foods – Who to promote?

CEO Colin Jones sat at his desk looking at a list of names. Jack Barnes, vice- president of sales, informed Colin two weeks prior that he was retiring. The five names on the list were possible successors to the vice president position. One of those candidates was Jane Jacob. There were many people in management who felt she was Big Deal Foods' rising star. Colin stared intently at Jane's name. There was a similar situation when Colin's dad Harper was CEO.

༄

Harper looked across his desk at Colin. Colin had just suggested Monica Goetting be promoted to Vice President of Special Products.

"Son," Harper began, "Goetting isn't vice president material. Yes, she's done good work and seems to be competent at what she does but a vice president needs to have mental toughness. It's not called the 'corporate jungle' for nothing. You have to be strong and balance the needs of the company before the needs of the self. What we need is a strong person who can make the tough calls when it matters most. Can't afford to look weak in business, son. Competitors think you're losing and stockholders lose confidence in you."

"How does that disqualify Monica Goetting?" Colin asked.

"How many jobs did your mother have? I'll tell you – one. Her job was to raise our children and make sure the household ran smoothly. She had her hands full just doing that. Goetting has kids. She'll be overwhelmed trying to juggle two jobs. She'll get distracted any time her kids get a runny nose. A vice president needs laser-like focus, tunnel vision, to be successful. Goetting has all she can handle as it is."

Colin understood. Goetting – along with any woman who would follow her – was not to be promoted beyond middle management.

Colin looked again at Jane Jacob's name. "A vice president needs to be focused. Can't afford to look weak," Colin said to himself.

Two floors below, Jane Jacob was talking with her colleague Devon Michaels.

"Word is you're on the short list for Barnes' job," Devon said.

"Well, that's all it will be – words," Jane retorted. "In the history of Big Deal Foods there has never been a female vice president. The employee handbook reads 'all qualified individuals will be considered for promotion'. That's true to a certain extent. But if you're a woman, middle management is as high as you'll ever be promoted. Besides, remember when the vice presidents and corporate officers had their 'special meeting' at the gentlemen's club? You think they'll want a woman in their club? Right."

"Some of that crap has to change," Devon replied. "Why not now? Why not you? What you need is someone on the inside to help you."

Jane shrugged her shoulders and walked back to her office. *"Maybe I should just start over somewhere else,"* she thought.

"It was the first time I experienced a situation over which I had no control. . .I was married, and it was an unwritten rule that to take a male client to a late lunch or supper was an absolute 'no-no.' Even if my boss took me to a noon luncheon it had to include at least one other lady from the office."

– Helen Shoars

Reflections Under Glass

*"People worried about a male lawyer and female lawyer travel-
ing together or being seen having lunch together...or being seen having
lunch or dinner together. What surprised lawyers was not that their wives
complained about the fact that their husbands were working with a young
woman. But they basically told me: 'My wife is all over me. For years I've
told her she can't have a career and a family, that she had to choose. And
here you are, you've got both, and she feels like I sold her a bill of goods.'
It was funny that [the wives] got upset with the husbands, not with me."*

Martha Barnett, American Bar Association President (2000-
2001)

*"You have to play by men's rules, but that doesn't mean you must be
domineering."*

Margaret "Peggy" Wolff, senior partner at Skadden, Arps,
Slate, Meagher

*"I know that it's difficult to balance a family and a research career in
science, with irregular schedules and 10- to 12-hour workdays. I see how
the women — and the men — in my lab struggle. I don't know if there's a
right time to do things in life, but I think there's probably a right time for
each person. I think the women who make it work in life and in the lab
have great partners. And I think women have to be very, very, very, flexible
to make it all work."*

Renee Reijo Pera, Infertility researcher, UCSF

"My job is sport. I play to win and I seek to dominate. Use your anger effectively by saying, 'I'm gonna beat that guy'."

Barbara Moakler Byrne, former managing director of Lehman Brothers

Glass Ceiling Reinforcement Terminology

On ramping – women wishing to return to work after career pauses.

Organizational culture – refers to the dominant attitudes, assumptions, and actions that represent the core values shared by most of the organization's members.

Social closure – individuals who observe and support those roles are ones that will be looked upon with favor, while those who go against tradition will be looked upon with disfavor and treated accordingly.

Societal roles – tell us how each gender should act and what activities are acceptable for each.

Shared values – refer to appropriate actions and standards of conduct by members of the organization as judged by those members.

Unwritten rules –behavioral constraints imposed in organizations that are not voiced or written down.

Written rules – all the formal, official, and understood aspects of the business. These written rules include vision statements, organizational charts, and policies.

Zero sum **game** – describes a situation in which a participant only gains at the expense of another participant – or when a loss by any participant benefits another participant.

5 KNOWLEDGE UNSHARED IS WORTHLESS

Women in power positions need to personally undertake efforts to assist other women in clearing organizational obstacles. Women trying to advance themselves professionally have a difficult time doing so when faced with rules and power structures designed and regulated by men. Female executives need to set an example among all executives to groom potential executives and to spotlight a largely untapped talent pool within the organization. A well-placed, successful, encouraging mentor can be your champion if you want to get noticed by the higher-ups but don't have the stomach to let everyone know how great you are. The challenge for women is to change the context in which they are seen and evaluated. Changing perceptions is one of the many things mentoring and feminism seek to accomplish.

Mentoring

Mentoring in an organization is a private relationship between two individuals based on a mutual desire for development toward an organizational objective. The mentoring relationship does not involve formal reporting and in no way infringes on any of the organization's existing communication channels, protocol, or hierarchical structures. A mentor is defined as an experienced, productive manager who relates well to a less-experienced employee and facilitates his or her personal development for the benefit of the individual and the organization.

Mentoring counters the internal forces of power positions and organizational culture by debunking stereotypes regarding the competency of women for executive-level positions and challenging the perceived "acceptable roles" for women. Protégées' abilities, competency, and versatility are showcased to the mentor.

Personal and professional growth are enhanced by the mentor. Protégées are able to build a network of at least one influential executive who, at the very least, could be used as a reference on a resume'.

Often the protégée attracts the attention of the mentor through outstanding job performance or similarity in interests or hobbies. A mentor promotes self-efficacy and expectations of success if the mentoring experience is based on the mentored woman's worldview. A mentor may help a protégée to see beyond her sexual and ethnic stereotypes in developing her self-awareness.

For a man, mentoring relationships offer ways to work toward his dream of corporate domination through the role-modeling, advice and counsel, and sponsorship he receives as a young adult striving to establish a satisfying career. For a woman, the dream tends to take a different form. Relationships, particularly with family, are central for women and interwoven with images of achievement.

Mentoring to success is, as yet, a largely unexplored arena for organizations. Within the context of relationships and achievement, mentoring can be particularly beneficial for women and organizations as a whole. Companies like Fannie Mae have discovered that mentoring is good for business. At Fannie Mae, women account for 60% of the participants in their mentoring program. Fannie Mae mentoring program manager Cecilia Blacutt:

"A main goal of our program is to advance highly qualified employees, particularly women and minorities. Our program provides the opportunity to develop skills and address personal and professional growth. Mentoring helps employees work smarter, develop themselves and become better at their jobs. And this means more productivity and happier employees to Fannie Mae."

Favoritism is a problem because it has been used in selecting men for executive positions. It is challenging for women to find mentors because mentors often select protégés who are like them.

Because senior leaders are men, they are more likely to select and groom men in the organization rather than women. Though mentoring programs pose significant challenges for organizations, the organization is better off with mentoring than without. Aspiring radio executive and glass ceiling research participant Bethany:

> "[Mentoring] has [helped in the radio industry] and because they [mentors] have helped me with skills that I hadn't developed that I needed to develop before I could move forward. It's interesting because it has also given me a confidence that I didn't necessarily have. That has helped me. I have much more confidence in my day-to-day work, and my ability to get to where I need to be."

Glass ceilings constitute a real limit to women's power, restricting their ability to provide instrumental types of mentoring, especially compared to what male peers can offer. The assumption that male mentors are better able to sponsor and promote has *some* basis in fact. As long as senior women are kept absent from the executive suite, they will be limited by their lack of access to senior management consideration, and by their limited ability to move junior women ahead.

Women, being members of the out-group – the subordinate, non-dominant group – find the focus on their own upward battle and blocked progress, leaving little time and energy to mentor. Instead, women have to work at building alliances with their seniors, regularly demonstrating their loyalty and competence, and making sure they are not sabotaged by the very subtle dynamics that keep the glass ceiling difficult to penetrate. Another factor inhibiting female mentors is that males hold more centralized, critical positions that give them access to valuable information concerning job openings, pending projects, and managerial decisions often shared through the "old boy network".

Women often receive more promotions than men, but are not advancing as far in the organizational hierarchy. The positive relationship between access to the dominant coalition and promotion

suggests that women who do not have a mentor may not be visible
to organizational decision makers. Being less visible reduces their
chances of promotions and job transfers.

The underlying issues reinforcing the male in-groups and female out-groups block mentoring relationships for women. There
are two primary forms of mentoring – grooming-mentoring and
networking-mentoring. The contrast between the two not only has
an impact on the effectiveness of mentoring women but also getting
more women into the "very high places" Susan Estrich talks about.

Grooming-mentoring and networking-mentoring

Grooming-mentoring is the special assistance provided by an
older, more experienced professional who grooms his or her
protégé during a transitional period. This assistance enhances fast
movement up the career ladder for a protégé. Grooming-mentoring has several distinctive characteristics. First, it has a developmental pattern. The mentor works one on one with the protégé
to impart specific knowledge and develop skills the protégé needs
to learn to advance within a particular vocation or area within an
organization. Second, grooming-mentoring relationships tend to
be homogeneous because mentors are likely to choose protégés
who are similar to them. Third, grooming-mentoring is based on
favoritism because mentors commit their resources to promoting
their protégés over others. Finally, grooming-mentoring is characterized by intense relationships.

Networking-mentoring, by contrast, entails more flexible
and mutually interdependent patterns of training, information
sharing, and support. Networking-mentoring is characterized
by a series of contacts between two or more people in which
each plays the role of mentor and protégée at different times and
to different degrees. Therefore, networking-mentoring is based
on the idea of mutual enhancement of careers and does not share
characteristics of grooming-mentoring such as developmental
stages, homogeneity, and intensity. Networking-mentoring

provides more than one mentor for the protégée, which is important for many reasons. Networking-mentoring provides a protégée with the ability to:

- Expand the base of authority figures from which to gain advocates within an organization and/or industry to aid in career advancement;
- Gain multiple perspectives;
- Not be dependent upon a single individual and trying to fit time into the mentor's schedule;
- Diminish generational differences that could stymie a one-on-one mentor/protégée relationship not present with peer pals.

Due to the mutuality involved, those who engage in networking-mentoring are not called mentors and protégées. They are instead called "peer pals" or simply "peers" to distinguish the various primary functions that peers can perform in networking- mentoring. There are three types of peers:

1. an information peer, who shares information
2. a collegial peer, who assists in planning career strategies and gives job-related feedback
3. a special peer, who provides emotional support and personal feedback.

The most important advantage of networking-mentoring is its availability to all women, not just the chosen few who can find someone to groom them. The other advantages of networking-mentoring:

- fewer relational problems that stem from intensity,
- greater self-reliance,
- less resentment by colleagues concerning favoritism, and
- less reliance on personal career success being dependent upon the mentor's career success.

An important distinction exists not only between the two types of mentoring (grooming versus networking) but also who does the mentoring (men versus women). Gender schemas affect how men in clout title positions view, evaluate, and reward the professional performance for women. Mentors should be advocates for the advancement of their protégées. Male mentors aren't effective mentors and advocates if they believe their female protégées are not competent for clout title positions.

Networking-mentoring and female-centered mentoring are more effective and beneficial models for women. Is there a difference in aspiring female executives being mentored by women as being mentored by men? The answer is yes. Aspiring radio executive and glass ceiling research participant Eleanor:

"[The male mentor was] not quite as patient. There is a difference [between male-centered and female-centered mentoring]. The difference is you're getting a female perspective versus a male's perspective, those two perspectives are totally different. A female will tell you the pitfalls of being a woman in the business and what to look out for. A man won't see that side of it. A man will be a lot more aggressive whereas a female may be more passive.

Aggressive in the sense that 'here's how you do the job, here's how you get the task done.' Whereas [with female mentors] I've seen and what I've experienced personally I've seen more 'here's how you have to do it, if this doesn't work then go about it this way'."

In Eleanor's experience, male mentors were task oriented, contrasted by female mentors being more sympathetic and steering a protégée in the right direction and more concerned about being flexible and open to more than one process being the correct one given the situation. These are two of the many advantages of female-centered mentoring.

Women who are mentored by men will gain benefit from the experiences. However, women who are mentored by other women are more likely to enhance and expand career skills, advance in their careers, receive higher salaries, and enjoy their work more. Both female mentors and their protégées say the relationship increases self-esteem and social connection. Another benefit for female protégées is that women mentors, having dealt with similar questions of identity, may be better able to support them in their struggles to find a satisfying work/life balance and realize their dreams. This is another reason why female-centered mentoring (women mentoring women) is more effective than male-centered mentoring (men mentoring women). Aspiring radio executive and glass ceiling research participant Danielle:

"She was the vice-president of sales in New York for one of the bigger companies, and she was awesome, and she got up [to speak during an industry seminar] and said, 'When I have sales people that are complaining about how they work too much and this too much and that too much, and I've been up since five in the morning getting my kids ready, and I've lucky if I don't have spit up on my clothes, my suit, when I get to work'...it put everything in perspective."

The career and psychological benefits women obtain from a mentoring relationship increase the likelihood that they will receive the support and cooperation of peers and subordinates. Female-centered mentoring increases protégées' self-esteem and social connection by having a female mentor as an advocate, allowing networking inside or outside the organization, and building alliances on the protégées' behalf. These benefits increase the protégées probability of success in the organization. Also, mentoring reduces job stress experienced by professional women who frequently do not have a peer group within the organization to rely on for psychological support.

Women who have one or more mentors reported greater job success and job satisfaction than women who did not have a mentor. Women whose worldview is one of collaboration find increased comfort with their organization when they have female mentors who have a similar worldview. The support that protégées have from their female mentors allows them to be more concerned about developing interpersonal and task-oriented skills rather than focusing on the lack of opportunities to be promoted to supervisory positions. Aspiring radio executive and glass ceiling research participant Bethany:

"With regard to superiors and managers, having this breadth of mentoring from high-powered women in the radio industry helped me to see managers more as peers, even though they're not. [Mentoring] helped me to see them on kind of a similar level because I was able to learn about a lot of these people's experiences, how they got to where they are and realizing that every one of these people that's my superior was at one point or another in my position or in a similar position to mine and, even though they're in a management position now, from a who they are standpoint, they're not all that much different."

Both grooming-mentoring and networking-mentoring are effective methods with which to help employees achieve career goals. The mentor adds instant credibility to the promising executive in the eyes of promotion-deciding executives. The mentor becomes an internal champion for the protégée. This internal champion fights for and argues on behalf of the protégée. It is vital for women to have a network of "internal champions," given the lack of women in clout title positions across the business landscape. The difference with the "internal champions" of networking-mentoring is the definition of "internal": in this case promising women executives might have to change organizations within the same industry. Internal champions are industry champions.

When it comes to mentoring, female mentors have an advantage over their male counterparts. This advantage can be summed up in one word: balance. Women are better at helping other women in providing perspective on balancing life issues in both the public and private skies. Glass ceiling research participant Cecille:

"Men don't go on maternity leave. Men manage men and other women and that's just kind of our culture. Women haven't always managed men. You have so many things in common that a male wouldn't have gone through…managing your family. Managing your time. How to get the most out of your career while raising our children. Having your children. Raising them. I don't think a man is in the same situation that can really understand that. Or very few."

If someone in an individual's network has clout or a clout title position, the better the chance that individual receives a desired position or promotion. This strategy is true regardless of gender; however, for women in non-traditional industries, networking becomes even more critical. Networking in and out of the workplace has been a strategy for business people to enhance their careers. The adage 'it's not what you know, it's who you know' becomes the mantra for someone seeking to move up the corporate ladder. The good news is that networking is not about schmoozing but about building genuine, meaningful relationships that enhance personal and professional growth. These skills can be learned and polished. In today's digital age, networking has never been easier. Social networking sites such as Facebook™ and professional networking sites such as LinkedIn™ have made it easy for people to connect with people who share common interests or pursuits. Vanessa DiMauro, CEO of Leader Networks:

"Through the growing use of social media for professional collaboration, there is an opportunity for women to change this trend by using social media to forge new connections, collaborate more with peers, and activate their network when seeking to advance."

Networking with female mentors in non-traditional career fields provides protégées a better perspective on positive shortcuts to success and how to avoid potential pitfalls or how to overcome pitfalls when they are encountered. Aspiring radio executive and glass ceiling research participant Eleanor:

*"I knew that these are dynamic women that could mentor me and give
me solid direction, help me through any kind of current challenges that
I was dealing with at that particular time, and those were the people to
know. And it was also an element of networking."*

As the protégées continue to climb corporate ladders, they
should consider creating a personal board of directors. This board
of directors is a source for career advice and guidance once a mentoring program ends. Business consultant Richard Leider recom-
mends contacting four to six people from which to learn from and
benefit from their wisdom.

The board should not only include friends and family members; Leider says the board should include a diverse group that
can pose the big questions that need to be asked. The composition
of the personal board of directors should feature a clarifier who
asks clear questions, a connector who leads you to other people,
a challenger who helps you act boldly, and a wise elder or sage.
Individuals need to draw upon the wisdom of people with diverse
perspectives who think differently than the individual does.

Thanks to technology, meetings with a personal board of
directors take place via telephone, e-mail, and live chats, although
occasional face-to-face meetings are beneficial. The protégées are
wise to employ their vast network for career advancement but
select an elite group of advocates to comprise their personal board
of directors for their long-term career success.

When it comes to deconstructing glass ceilings, mentoring
helps to change the perception of how women are seen and evaluated in the workplace by those executives who make decisions
regarding promotions. Feminism seeks to shape society's perception regarding women having equal access to the public sky and
how best to make that access a reality.

Feminism
Feminism has been defined "any attempt to improve the lot of any
group of women through female solidarity and a female perspec-

tive." Feminism has sought to shape and reflect how women have viewed themselves as wives, mothers, and workers. It has considered how and why women have accepted or rejected their roles within society and their own individual families.

One of the main objectives of feminist self-determination is creating a society that allows both women and men to determine and implement their own goals. Most feminists do not want to be the target or the cause of oppressive power, but instead value empowerment, internal strength, and self-determination that are hindered when power differentials exist. This distinction among feminists, between "empowerment from within" versus "power from without," has been characterized as "power to" as opposed to "power over."

The freedom and autonomy of empowered individuals do not exist at the expense of others. Feminism's value system involves the denial of using power to dominate others. This decision not to dominate others flies in the face of what women encounter in a male-dominated power structure in today's society. Present-day feminists combine personal and social change in virtually all ways to develop an agenda for the movement. Women must overcome sexist oppression by changing and reorganizing – not destroying – society. Though each of the feminist voices make these claims, the way each voice speaks and seeks remedy to the inequality varies from voice to voice.

"Therefore, it is necessarily a struggle to eradicate the ideology of domination that permeates Western culture on various levels, as well as a commitment to reorganizing society so that the self-development of people can take precedence over imperialism, economic expansion, and material desires."
– *Bell Hooks*

Feminism opposes the external factors of gender and societal roles by challenging society's perceptions about women in business having a corner office. Feminists share a common goal of ending sexist oppression but not all feminists agree on the role men should play in assisting to end that oppression. If women are to advance into clout title positions in male-dominated industries, women won't be able to do it alone. Women and men holding clout title positions need to encourage and assist promising women who seek to climb corporate ladders. The probability of deconstructing glass ceilings is greater if coalitions of men and women work together. Diane K. Danielson, President of the Downtown Women's Club:

"I would also recommend expanding your network beyond women. Men still make up the majority of board positions and you'll need to convince them that you should be serving. It may be hard to just jump on a board-especially a public one. You might start small with non-profits or an alumni board and then build up."

However, not all women feel this way. There are some women who believe that the oppressors – men – are the problem and cannot be part of the solution. Do the oppressed women have a better view of reality, which seems to suggest that oppression should be maintained, lest the oppressed lose their clear vision from below the liberated? There is a school of thought that believes only women can help women and the oppressor cannot help the oppressed. Their view is flawed because this view, taken to a similar conclusion, would hold that white women need to be silenced in order to listen to black women.

So, is there room for men in the feminist movement…can men be feminists? Absolutely. Feminism is not a single point of view but a set of principles for interpreting the status of women and demanding change. There is no biological or psychological trait that makes it absolutely impossible for men with different or comparable experiences to sympathize with oppressed women. Neither is there any innate quality that commands automatic identification from all women with all women, give the varying ideologies, social situations, contexts, and levels of consciousness of women.

Men should not be seen as the standard against which women are to be measured for equal justice. The standard for measurement should be what is moral, just, and within the letter and spirit of our laws. Equality does not mean equality of outcomes; it means equality of opportunities. If more women had equal opportunities to be eligible for clout title positions, a major step toward equality would be achieved.

Susan Estrich believes the most important step to getting more women into very high places in the workplace or in politics is just getting more women in the room. When there is only one woman in the room, the chance that all women will fail is too high, and the burden on the one who's trying can be insurmountable. As Joan Gerberding pointed out, getting more women in the pipeline is not the answer to the problem. There can be a significant number of women in the pipeline but that pipeline is getting choked off before women reach the highest levels of business. Getting more women in the room, rather than more women in the pipeline, should be the priority.

The feminist movement has tried to improve and reform society to fit its vision of what a just society should be. The basic questions feminists ask focus on whether women and men are so different that those differences justify unequal treatment in employment and before the law. Feminists have worked in the political arena in order to get legislation passed to help level the playing field for women and not just in the workplace. Title IX and EEO laws have assisted women in getting closer to competing with men or having similar opportunities as men do in business or college athletics. The problem with those laws is that they aren't necessarily focused on people but on numbers.

EEO legislation, for example, considers only how many women are employed or recruited, not how many women are in certain positions of authority. Women are employed and recruited for entry-level and mid-level positions in companies but not for the clout level positions. The letter of the law has been satisfied, but not its spirit. If women are to achieve clout title positions, they must find allies and employ methods on local (company) and regional (industry) levels rather than global (government-mandated) levels.

Does a female-centered, networking-mentoring program exist that allows protégées to develop a network of influential executives? Yes. An organization known as Mentoring and Inspiring Women (MIW) created a female-centered mentoring initiative to assist women with executive ambitions in the male-dominated radio industry. The example set by MIW is one that is enhancing opportunities for its protégées. The MIW mentoring program is one that should be replicated by other industries, particularly those that are traditionally male-dominated. Chapter Six will examine this ground-breaking networking-mentoring initiative.

Big Deal Foods – Won't You Be My Mentor?

Six months after being passed over for the vice-president position, Jane Jacob sat in her office. She was a person who kept up on industry trends and news. Shortly after not getting the vice-president's position, Jane saw a press release regarding a group of influential women in the food industry starting a mentoring program for women looking to advance to clout title positions. Jane went to the web site listed in the press release and saw details on how the program worked and how to apply for the mentorship program. The criteria to be eligible for the mentoring program:

- employed a minimum of five years in the food processing industry,
- hold a director or management level position,
- agree to actively participate in the mentoring process and,
- agree to total confidentiality during the mentoring program.

Applicants were also required to submit a letter addressing the question, "Why would I be a good mentee?" Jane had the qualifications to apply for the program and did so.

"*Now we'll see if I get selected*," Jane thought.

Two months later.

Jane was at her desk working when her phone rang. Two rings later, she answered it. "Jane, this is Sylvia Marcotte," the voice on the other end greeted. "I wanted to call to tell you the good news that you've been selected to be one of our mentees for this year." Jane was not only happy to be selected but that it was Sylvia, *the Sylvia Marcotte*, calling her personally. Sylvia Marcotte was one of the food processing industry's biggest stars…the CEO of Rival Foods. Jane thanked Sylvia for the opportunity.

Sylvia continued, "Starting Friday, Team Jane will hold a weekly noon conference call. There are five of us on your team who will be on the call each week for the first quarter. In subsequent quarters, the members of Team Jane will change so you have the chance to be mentored by all the members of our group. I am the chairperson of Team Jane. I will facilitate each conference call. My advice to you is that each week between calls you keep notes of any questions or challenges you have so that you're prepared to bring them up before the Team. We are here to be not only your mentoring team but your support system as well. There may be things that you're encountering that we have dealt with as well. Feel free to shoot us an email with questions too."

"How will I know who to ask a specific question to best take advantage of each team member's experiences?" Jane inquired.

"That's where I come in," Sylvia replied. "If you email me your question first, I can direct you to the person best able to give you the guidance you're seeking. Don't be surprised if

Team Jane members refer you to other members of the group or other industry people they know for a particular question or concern you have. That's what we're here for…to help you the best we can to further your career through our network. The first thing you need to do is to complete the questionnaire I'm going to email you shortly. We need to know what challenges you're facing as you start this mentoring program and what areas you'd like to Team Jane to focus on as we begin our time together."

"I'll have that questionnaire back to you by tomorrow afternoon," Jane said.

"I'm looking forward to our first Team Jane meeting," Sylvia replied.

The call ended. Jane couldn't help but feel the adrenaline rushing through her system. "*Team Jane,*" she mused. "*I like that.*"

Three months following the start of her mentoring experience, Jane's career satisfaction had never been higher. Her job satisfaction was acceptable but now Jane felt as though she had options, that her career success or failure was not directly dependent upon Big Deal Foods anymore. It didn't matter if she could crack the glass ceiling here. She had formed her own industry network through Team Jane. If a job came open elsewhere, not only would her team inform her of the opening, but would openly advocate for her to get the position. There were no guarantees, of course, but that was a huge step up the ladder for Jane.

Jane's time as a mentee had helped her at Big Deal Foods as well. Jane was not shy about calling her Team members when faced with a situation at Big Deal Foods she had not seen before. In each instance Jane's mentor(s) advised her in the right direction or supplied the physical or mental tools to assist Jane make the best decision possible. Jane's ability to relate and to delegate duties to her subordinates increased. She learned that she didn't have to shoulder everything, that if she mentored the people in her department, they were more productive and effective in their respective jobs.

Now ten months into the program, Team Jane was in its last quarter. Jane Jacob was now with her fourth, and final, mentoring committee. Jane had mixed feelings. She was a little sad her time with these women was almost done but jubilant at the same time because of what these women had helped her accomplish.

Through the guidance of the Team Jane members and Jane's hard work and dedication, Jane Jacob was Big Deal Foods' shining star. Productivity, efficiency, and job satisfaction among those in her department were the highest in the company. Jane's last performance review was the best she'd ever had at Big Deal Foods. Jane's direct report asked her during the review if the mentoring program was part of the reason for her success. "Absolutely," Jane said.

In the end, Jane got a substantial raise but, again, was passed over when a vice-president's position came open. She was disappointed but not devastated. One of her Team Jane members had recommended Jane to the CEO of Limitless Foods. Impressed with Jane's credentials, track record, and glowing reports from industry insiders, the CEO of Limitless Foods offered her, and Jane accepted, the position of Vice-President of Special Projects.

Jane was grateful for what Team Jane had done for her. As a result, Jane did two things: she became a member of the influential women of the food processing industry and became a mentor. Other women had paid it forward. Now Jane would too.

"Liberation" meant empowerment. I was empowered to throw a 50-pound sack of flour on my shoulder and carry it for customers. I was empowered to throw the deck in a semi-tractor trailer. I was empowered to eviscerate 30-pound turkeys. I was empowered to drive a school bus when there were only two of us women driving in the whole school district at the time. Our men co-drivers were always helpful and respectful. I have worked right beside men all my life; always, always with equal pay and advancement. I never considered myself unequal to men and I never will."

– Helen Shoars

Reflections Under Glass

"Women have not had enough 'locker room talk'...We need to build these networks, to work together to advance our careers and improve our skills. Whether the mentoring is formal or informal, mentoring helps you make better choices, get objective feedback and get connected so you can move ahead in your career."
Mary Fran, Director of New Media at Fannie Mae

"Well if women don't mentor other women, who will?...We have an obligation to help women get where they want to be. I call the highest ranking woman in any organization I deal with so she is sure to be acknowledged for the business we help her deliver in that organization."
Michele Hughes, Executive Director of The Anne Arundel County YWCA [in 2002]

"Feminists changes have made it easier for my daughter to have broader choices than women had growing up when feminism was in its insurgency. She knows she has work options if she chooses them, options that the 1950s generation of mothers did not have. But she has no illusions about what it means to be a working mother. A pressured and stressful job can't compete in the quality of life categories with cooking for her husband and son."
Suzanne Fields, Columnist.

Glass Ceiling Deconstruction Terminology

Female-centered mentoring – any mentoring program where women mentor women.

Feminism – any attempt to improve the lot of any group of women through female solidarity and a female perspective.

Grooming-mentoring – the special assistance provided by an older, more experienced professional who grooms his or her protégé during a transitional period.

Mentoring – a private relationship between two individuals based on mutual desire for development toward an organizational objective.

Networking-mentoring – characterized by a series of contacts between two or more people in which each plays the role of mentor and protégée at different times and to different degrees.

Personal board of directors – a pool of four to six people who act as a source of career advice and guidance once a mentoring program ends.

6 ROCK STARS

While discrimination against women in all industries is a public policy concern, the role of women in commercial radio companies is of particular interest because the radio industry plays a special role in society. The news and entertainment content on commercial radio not only tells the public about the events of the day, but also tells the public about itself. Radio influences public thought about issues and attitudes in our society and communicates in subtle ways who and what is important and normal – men in clout positions – and who has status and power – men, not women.

The majority of ultimate radio decision-makers regarding programming, content, and editorial decisions in the general media are men. They affect the promotion prospects of many women who aspire to senior positions. Women don't reach the top, in part, because of male attitudes. The most common obstacle to career development reported by women journalists is male attitudes toward women in the media.

Women hold only 16.8% of all general manager positions in the top 100 radio markets, and only 33.2% of sales manager jobs. Women in the radio industry are most likely to be found working as salespeople or as on-air personalities but not as frequently in executive levels of management. Women sales managers are more common within the radio industry than are women program directors, general managers or market managers. The radio industry is subject to the influence of the broader society in which only two percent of CEOs in the Fortune 1000 are female.

Out of the 120 radio ownership groups owning 12 or more commercial radio stations, 18.5% of the 4,814 stations owned by these groups are managed by women. Entercom (24% managed by women), Clear Channel (20%), Citadel (19%) are above the industry average, while Cumulus (17% managed by women), and

Infinity (15%) are slightly below the industry average. However, the more telling number is this: 42 groups, including Jefferson-Pilot, Greater Media, Nassau Broadcasting, New Northwest, and Mid-West Family *have no female general managers*. 42 (35%) of the 120 radio ownership groups have no women in those positions. That number reflects the national ownership groups and doesn't take into account the nearly 7,186 remaining commercial radio stations in the United States.

These numbers give us a clear indication of the height of radio's glass ceilings. Those ceilings appear to be higher among Entercom, Clear Channel, and Citadel; a little lower between Cumulus and Infinity; and extremely low among the rest of the consolidated ownership groups. Glass ceilings are alive and well in the radio industry.

Radio is no different than most industries in that there is a perception that it's "an old boys club" and that women are treated differently than men. This is especially true the higher up the corporate ladder women attempt to climb. Wherever one looks in the world, women still have relatively little decision-making power either inside the media organizations themselves, or in the political and economic institutions with which these organizations must interface. It is as if one woman at the top is as much as the system can absorb without being thrown into a paroxysm of pro-fessional anguish about the potential effects – on status, salaries, and self-esteem – of feminization.

Another obstacle for women in radio is that consolidation of radio station ownership has dramatically changed the industry. The number of "mom and pop" owned radio stations has decreased significantly while the number of stations owned by large corpo-rate groups has risen. Now that publicly traded companies own large numbers of radio properties, the nature of the business has changed to one that is primarily driven by the bottom line and stock prices. This has created a change in the culture of the indus-try and the individual radio stations.

The passage of the Telecommunications Act of 1996 changed
the way radio does business and has had an impact on the values
created, maintained, and enforced by the leaders of the industry.
Included in the Telecom Act was the lifting of ownership limits for
the radio industry. Before the Act, there were a limited number
of radio stations an individual person or group could own. Since
the passage of the Act, ownership groups such as Clear Channel,
Cumulus, Infinity, Radio One, and Emmis have acquired hundreds
– and, in Clear Channel's case, thousands – of radio stations across
the country. Most of these radio ownership groups are publicly-
traded companies. Thus, two values that are closely maintained in
today's radio industry are to keeping stock prices high and keeping
shareholders happy. Clear Channel's CEO Mark P. Mays:

*"We have a common culture in the company. We are all here to en-
hance shareholder value. You have to think of that as number one. I tell
people, if they are not enhancing shareholder value somehow, then their job
is not going to be around much longer. That goes for everyone, from the
corporate office to someone answering the phone at a station."*

The preceding quote came from Mr. Mays while Clear Channel
Communications was still a publicly-traded company. As of 2008,
Clear Channel is a privately-held company.

Consolidation caused the number of radio sales people to mul-
tiply while the number of middle and upper level executive positions has declined. Before 1996, if a particular city had eight radio
stations in the market, eight of those stations could have been
owned by four different ownership interests – whether "mom and
pop" or corporation – because regulations limited how many stations one ownership interest could possess within defined geo-
graphic or population areas. Since consolidation, one ownership
group can own over half of those eight stations in our hypothetical
market, meaning fewer managers overseeing more radio stations.

Before Consolidation there may have been a general manager for each of the stations in a market. Now there's a general

manager – or market manager – overseeing all of the stations
within a particular ownership group. More than a decade after
Consolidation, it is more difficult than ever for women to achieve
clout title positions because now there are even fewer of those
positions to be had. Executive Vice-President and Chief Operating Officer of GreenStone Media, LLC Edie Hilliard:

> *"If success is defined as having the most stations or the most money
> and, therefore, the most power, then, no, women do not have as fair a
> chance to be successful in our business as men do. With consolidation,
> management opportunities for women are shrinking."*

There is a powerful group of women in the radio industry
working to get more women in executive positions. This group
– Mentoring and Inspiring Women – has undertaken an initiative
to assist women to achieve clout title positions. This initiative
contains a blueprint for women of all industries to emulate and
implement in order for women to break through glass ceilings,
regardless of the size, shape, scope, or height of those ceilings.

Mentoring and Inspiring Women started as the Most Influential Women in Radio, originating in the pages of *Radio Ink* magazine. In 1999 *Radio Ink* introduced a feature called, "The Most
Influential Women in Radio" to identify those women whose leadership and dedication have guided and changed the radio industry,
but also to hammer more cracks in radio's glass ceiling. A handful of those initial 20 women featured in 1999 founded the MIW
group. There are now 61 MIW members. MIW is committed to
using its influence and resources to help put more women in positions of leadership in the radio industry, on broadcasting company
boards, and on boards of radio associations.

The members of Mentoring and Inspiring Women have spent
their professional lives trying to attain clout title positions. The
Mentoring and Inspiring Women group is comprised of top-level
radio women across the country committed to using their influence and resources to support other women in radio to develop

strong management and leadership skills. The MIWs are equally committed to advocating the advancement of women to senior positions in radio companies and corporations. MIW has chosen to adopt a grassroots initiative within the industry to break radio's glass ceilings rather than relying on the legislative process to level the playing field.

The MIW's strategy to accomplish its mission is through a group-mentoring program. The networking-mentoring program is for women in the radio industry who wish to advance to executive levels of management. Each year the group selects three to four women to be its protégées. The differences between this mentoring program and traditional mentoring programs are that the protégées have access to all 61 MIWs as mentors rather than just one person and all of the mentors are women.

Female-centered mentoring – women mentoring women – has a greater impact on mentoring for women than male-centered mentoring – men mentoring women. Studies reveal that women who are mentored by other women in either grooming-mentoring or networking-mentoring situations are more likely to enhance and expand career skills, advance in their careers, receive higher salaries, and enjoy their work more. Mentors and protégées believe this relationship increases self-esteem and social connection.

The MIW group mentoring program was launched in 2002. The Mildred C. Carter MIW Group Mentoring Program is named in honor of a pioneering broadcaster who was one of the first African American female radio station owners and helped pave the way for women in radio.

The program's focus is to match protégées with female radio professionals who are leaders in the industry. The MIW group-mentoring program has assisted protégées with learning more about the ins and outs of the industry, networking up and down the corporate ladder, and providing guidance to grow their careers. Each December the MIWs choose three to four candidates from a pool of applicants from the radio broadcasting industry. Candidates from sales, programming, marketing and other related fields in radio broadcasting are encouraged to apply. Since 2002, the MIW Group has mentored 17 women, of which 11 have been promoted.

The mentoring applicants are required to be no less than director or manager level, but can encompass all areas and departments of radio station operations or related fields. All potential protégées are required to submit a letter that addresses the question: "Why would I be a good mentee?" Candidates for the MIW group mentoring program must also meet the following criteria:

- have been in the radio industry for five years or more,
- agree to actively participate in the mentoring process, and
- agree to total confidentiality during the mentoring program.

The process starts once the protégées have been selected and notified of their acceptance into the program. The first step in the mentoring process is for the MIWs to branch into four committees. One of the MIW members functions as committee chair for Team Protégée. The protégée then completes a questionnaire that elicits responses to target what specific areas the protégée wants to focus on as well as some challenges she's facing at the time. The MIWs review the questionnaire and then set up a schedule for conference calls with the mentor team.

Each of the teams mentors one of the selected protégées for three months. One of the MIWs acts as the team leader and initiates a conversation to discuss what the protégées' goals are for that quarter. On Fridays the protégée has a conference call with one of the MIWs on her mentor team. During the week the protégée will jot down any problems, questions, or concerns to bring up for discussion during the conference call. The protégée will seek the counsel of her MIW mentor during the weekly conference call. The individual mentor rotates each Friday, so the protégée talks with a different MIW each time. Any questions would not only be addressed by the mentors with possible solutions but a referral to an individual who specializes in a particular area. The mentors then determine when it is convenient for the protégée to make the call to that individual and provide the assistance needed. The advantages of this group mentoring program:

- Interacting between protégées and mentors allows for multiple perspectives;
- Networking is done with a broader base of influential people;
- Rotating mentors and protégées lessens chance of relationship breakdowns.

These advantages enable the MIW program to create stronger bonds between mentors and protégées, less friction due to workplace jealousies or politics, a wider base of experiences to draw from women who've gone through similar circumstances, and building an inner circle of industry peers who can refer or recommend protégées for open clout title positions.

I interviewed six of the nine protégées who had completed the MIW mentoring program at the time of my glass ceiling research. All of the interview participants were promised anonymity to ensure an open and safe dialogue. Radio is a small industry and, as women in a male-dominated field, candor could be a career killer. Therefore, the names appearing with their quotes are not their real names but pseudonyms.

Here is a brief introduction to the six MIW protégées I interviewed. Andrea is African American and has been in the radio for 16 years. Bethany is Caucasian and has been in radio for 28 years. Cecille is Caucasian and has been in the industry 18 and a half years. Eleanor is African American and has been in the industry 20 years. Faye is Caucasian and has been in the industry 25 years. Of all the interviewees, Eleanor is the only woman who does not have children. Their quotes allow us to see the various aspects of the constructing, reinforcing, and deconstructing panes of glass ceilings through the prism of their professional and mentoring experiences.

> *"It [MIW mentoring] was really a neat experience. I got to speak to these women who were...rock stars. In our business they were just so incredibly successful." — Cecille*

Constructing panes

Glass ceilings have been defined earlier as *invisible barriers in the workplace that prevent women from attaining clout title positions.* Historically, glass ceilings have been perceived as being a by-product of gender discrimination and gender stereotypes. I don't discount that gender discrimination and gender stereotypes play a role; however, they are not the be-all-end-all of what constructs and reinforces glass ceilings.

> *"Maybe I just didn't notice it before but to me it's gotten a lot worse than it was in the past or in my earlier career. Depending upon the company now, some avenues are just closed so one tends to go to the company that actually not just talks about diversity and opportunities for females, but actually have women in positions of leadership and there are many of those, not as many as there should be..."*
> *— Bethany*

MIW member Joan Gerberding told me that one of the biggest challenges for women is being perceived as a threat to other (male) managers, instead of someone who could help them achieve – or exceed – their goals. Positive leadership skills are not gender based; they are related to how women as managers choose to live their lives – both personally and professionally. Leadership skills, Gerberding expressed, are also about how leaders choose to incorporate and implement strategies or systems designed to increase productivity, develop improved processes for attracting, developing, retaining and utilizing people with the required skills and attitudes to meet business needs.

The women interviewed have taken ownership of their careers in pursuit of clout title positions. They are willing to invest their time and money to better themselves personally and professionally, beyond the MIW mentoring program. Andrea, Bethany, Cecille, and Danielle pointed out that their career goals include senior management positions such as president of a broadcast radio division, CEO of a radio company or outright ownership of their own station(s). Faye expressed a desire to be a sales manager.

Four of the six women specifically mentioned things they had done to improve their skills, including reading books, keeping up to date on industry developments through trade magazines, and attending Radio Advertising Bureau (RAB) and state broadcast association seminars. Each woman had strategies in mind to achieve their goals. The MIW mentoring program has been an important part of the goal achievement process.

"It's prepared me to achieve my career goals because I've been able to utilize this opportunity as networking which can help me in the future. It's helped me prepare myself with the day-to-day tasks, and it's helped me with dealing with gender imbalances and gender harassments and issues."
— *Eleanor*

"I don't have to recreate the wheel and it constantly reminds me that other people have treaded this path before...being part of the program has given me a broader scope of how to approach different situations."
— *Andrea*

"I have stayed in contact with many of those individuals, and they have been of great assistance and support and have given me guidance... and I have a good network of individuals that provide me with guidance and assistance."
— *Bethany*

"But knowing that there are so many successful women out there even though it's not the norm in the industry because it is kind of a man's world is very encouraging."
— Danielle

Achieving career goals is difficult for women when men set the standards for all promising executives to meet. Women are at a disadvantage because men are more likely to promote other men. Also, women may not believe the risks necessary to compete for those clout title positions are greater than the potential rewards. Power positions were viewed as a factor in constructing glass ceilings but not necessarily the most important factor.

Gender is one of the most readily available characteristics upon which to exclude others. Assumptions are made by those in power positions regarding the competence of women to handle certain levels of roles and responsibilities within an industry or individual organization.

Though none of the MIW protégées claimed to be a victim of "the system," each expressed a certain amount of frustration about how they are treated because they are women, and thus must learn unwritten rules and adapt to them in order to survive in the industry. Eleanor revealed during our conversation that she had filed a gender harassment claim a week prior to being interviewed. The MIW protégées also expressed how difficult it is to be taken seriously because they are women and, additionally, how it affects how they are perceived and treated as a result:

"My first job I worked for an ex-con — literally. Him [sic] and his wife owned the station, and he thought women were pretty much pieces of meat to be told what to do. So I learned a lot of what not to do and what not to tolerate in our business."
— Andrea

MIW member Joan Gerberding told me there have been a series of "breakthrough" moments during her 30-plus year career, but one in particular stands out. When she was in her 20s, Joan was promoted to general sales manager of a small FM radio station on Cape Cod, Massachusetts. When she called her parents to tell them the news, Joan's mom said "well, it's about time." At first Joan was taken aback by the comment. Her mother hadn't praised her, as Joan had expected. Joan realized later her mom was saying to her was that "of course you should be promoted because you can go anywhere you set your mind to go and you have the talent and skills to go anywhere." It changed Joan's thinking and her self-confidence forever.

Reinforcing panes

Once glass ceilings are constructed, they must be reinforced if those in power want to maintain the status quo in their organization and/or industry. Men in power positions create an organizational culture that defines behavior. This created culture reinforces the attitudes, beliefs, and perceptions of men in clout title positions. Societal roles are an extension of gender and how each gender is expected to act in social and work situations. Any person who fails to fulfill a societal role assigned to his or her gender is viewed negatively and evaluated unfavorably. Organizational culture and societal roles play a large part in keeping glass ceilings in place generation after generation.

Organizational culture is "a cognitive framework [which] consists of assumptions and values shared by organization members". Jerald Greenberg says organizational culture provides a sense of identity for its members, generates commitment to the organization's mission, and clarifies and reinforces standards of behavior. Organizational culture guides employees' words and deeds, making it clear what they should do or say in a given situation, thereby providing stability to behavior.

Andrea and Faye expressed how their organizations fostered cultures that maximized their skills, utilized their talents, and created an environment within which they thrive.

*"...it's been a long time since I have been in that type of an environ-
ment where they [company] say 'here are your skills, let's create something
so you can maximize your skills to help us better' so I will probably die
before I leave this group."*
— *Andrea*

*"He [the original general manager] really created the culture. He
started the radio station and developed that kind of family type of feeling
and really kind of embraced everybody that worked for him and when he
left the person that is now the general manager maintained that culture
because she knew how important that was to the people that worked there."*
— *Faye*

The subject of organizational culture also brought forth responses about the darker side of the industry and individual organizations, particularly for these women. Changes in the industry
regulations, the "good ole boys" dynamic, weekly work hours, and
compensation were illustrations given as to how organizational
culture can have a negative impact on organizations and women in
particularly.

*"It's everything from pay structure still to, you know, harassment in
the workplace unfortunately, too, you just don't see a lot of female general
managers out there. It's more men. When I go to sit in a meeting, and
I'm talking about a harassment issue, I'm sitting in that meeting and it's
all men that I'm talking to. And being a minority as a female sitting in a
room it's still very uncomfortable because a man, I don't believe, is going to
see the issues that a woman has just because it's a gender imbalance."*
— *Eleanor*

MIW member Erica Farber told me that when she started in
radio she was constantly told she "couldn't" because of her gender.
Erica said men could get away with that back then. When Erica
was given opportunities, the people passed over were very open

about their assumptions that the only way she could have gotten those opportunities was because it involved sexual favors. Erica says that if she'd actually had the "adventures" she was accused of having, it was amazing she survived let alone been able to show up for work every day.

Societal roles come from how adults teach children what it considers proper behavior for men and women in our society. Men and women alike can satisfy many roles – personal and professional. However, some roles women attempt to satisfy are frowned upon by men and/or society at large.

Women who try to fulfill more than one role find their lack of professional support a formidable obstacle in the workplace. Women striving to achieve clout title positions in the workplace, while also being wives and mothers, face difficult decisions. They must decide what has priority at a given moment and then face poor evaluation by those in clout title positions who may disagree with their priorities. If men in power positions believe women in their organization are placing too much weight on family or children's issues, they may mentally disqualify those women from future promotions.

The MIW mentees, for the most part, viewed their role as mothers complementary, not contradictory, to their professional one. These women feel there are challenges inherent in trying to fulfill those roles but held that it made them more complete individuals. Children, by and large, were viewed as a benefit, not a detriment to their careers. During my conversations with them, the key theme consistently expressed was *balance*.

"I am really a firm believer in a balance being an enhancement to the whole package of a human being. The fact that you have interests outside of work, the fact that you have family obligations...I think that just makes you a whole person."
— *Bethany*

"I have some pretty strong opinions on the challenges of females in management roles, it's not that big of a challenge when you don't have a family, but the challenges and balance become issues, and I think the people that you work for make the difference. I have been fortunate enough to have been able to grow and manage both my household and my job. That is a huge issue and I think that is why we have trouble finding female managers."
— Cecille

"I think it makes for a better life's balance, and I wouldn't have felt as fulfilled if all I had was a career and not a family as well. I really work towards a balance of career, family, and fun."
— Danielle

"I do not have any children. It's [career goals influencing when to have children] influenced it greatly. In fact, I sought out to work on my career and that was a choice… to go forward more on my career and then concentrate on family, unfortunately, as a [secondary choice]."
— Eleanor

The MIWs are proof that women can effectively handle both private and public skies. Work and life strategies are important concerns for women managing both skies. Female-centered mentoring coaches the whole woman, not just the professional one. Male-centered mentoring, traditionally, concerns itself with an individual's professional sphere. For women who are striving to balance work and family responsibilities, including both childbearing and childrearing, being tutored on life strategies in professional and personal roles becomes critically important. Female-centered mentoring is a crucial component as women attempt to reach the corner office.

Deconstructing panes

Mentoring is the deconstructing schema that opposes power positions and organizational culture. Allowing women access to mentors provides access to greater professional opportunities, whether inside an individual organization or an industry. While mentoring goes to the heart of improving the opportunities of those women seeking to achieve clout title positions within organizations, feminism goes to the heart of changing the attitudes, assumptions, and beliefs of society. It is feminism that opposes gender and societal role schemas and seeks to level the playing field for women by reshaping the mental models of women that men manufacture.

"Because I know I'm at where I am now because there was somebody who took the time to share information with me, and if that person didn't do it for me I wouldn't be where I'm at. I can't be selfish because I've been blessed to be where I'm at."
— *Andrea*

"These are women [MIW] that are basically there. They came, they saw, they conquered. I mean, they totally were at the level where I wanted to be at that particular time. So being able to talk with them gave me phenomenal insight."
— *Eleanor*

The MIWs have shown and modeled for their protégées that paving the way for other women is vital to help *all* women succeed. The protégées realize the impact mentors have and how important it is to be a mentor to other women. This concept became clear when the protégées realized the MIWs represent only a handful of women in the radio industry willing to show the way to other women. Though the 61 women in the MIW group do not represent all the women in the radio industry helping other women to achieve their career goals, they are the only women to do so with such a high profile initiative. The protégées indicated during our conversations that they perceive that some women are not receptive to helping other women because of the potential competitors the assistance would create.

The protégées are putting competitive self-interest aside so all women achieve.

"I can't be selfish because I've been blessed to be where I'm at now.   My next job is to help someone else get to where I'm at."
- Andrea

"I'm definitely inclined to be a mentor now and in the future because I do feel that I need to pay it forward, I need to pay back what I have re-ceived through that mentoring program from this group who mentored me."
— Bethany

The MIWs recognize and embrace their responsibility to assist other women to clout title positions and encourage their protégés to exemplify the "pay it forward" philosophy. That philosophy is one that should be embraced by women in other male-dominated industries as well.

The future
Though there are success stories among the protégées after participating in the MIW's mentoring program, the full effect on their careers will not be known for some time. Since 2002, 17 women have completed a female-centered mentoring program in an industry that is male top heavy. Statistically, this is a not a large sample. However, this endeavor is not about getting more women in the pipeline. The MIW mentoring program is about honing the skills of a select group of women who have the abil-ity, attitude, and desire to ascend to the highest peaks of radio's hierarchy and developing a road map to getting there. The MIW mentors and protégées are leading a revolution to demonstrate women add just as much value and provide as much leadership as men. The protégées, in turn, will mentor other aspiring women within their professional spheres to aid them in their quest for executive positions.

Beyond radio, the MIW mentoring initiative is one that other industries should consider replicating. In 2009, 15 Fortune 500 companies had female CEOs. 28 Fortune 1000 companies had female CEOs. Here is the list of the Fortune 1000 female CEOs and their company's ranking on the top 1000:

CEO	Company	Rank
Brenda C. Barnes	Sara Lee	199
Carol A. Bartz	Yahoo!	345
Angela F. Braley	WellPoint	32
Catherine M. Burzik	Kinetic Concepts	938
Lynn L. Eisenhans	Sunoco	56
Patricia Gallup	PC Connection	985
Christina A. Gold	Western Union	451
Ilene Gordon	Corn Products International	560
Mindy F. Grossman	HSN	714
Susan M. Ivey	Reynolds American	294
Andrea Jung	Avon Products	255
Katherine Krill	AnnTaylor Stores	846
Ellen Kullman	DuPont	75

CEO	Company	Rank
Linda A. Lang	Jack in the Box	685
Constance H. Lau	Hawaiian Electric Industries	655
Tamara L. Lundgren	Schnitzer Steel Industries	595
Carol M. Meyrowitz	TJX	131
Anne Mulcahy	Xerox	147
Indra K. Nooyi	PepsiCo	52
Janet L. Robinson	New York Times	697
Irene B. Rosenfeld	Kraft Foods	53
Mary F. Sammons	Rite Aid	100
Anne Stevens	Carpenter Technology	890
Cindy B. Taylor	Oil States International	698
Mary Agnes Wilderotter	Citizens Communications	834
Patricia A. Woertz	Archer Daniels Midland	27
Dona Davis Young	Phoenix	863

It would seem that women have never had it better in regard to breaking through male-dominated arenas. However, only two percent of America's Fortune 1000 CEOs are women. Two percent. This number does not take into account the other clout title positions such as COOs, CFOs, presidents, and vice-presidents. However, the number does illustrate our society has a long way to go before women are truly holding up half of the public sky. Female-centered mentoring programs among the Fortune 1000 companies would be a way for pioneering women in all industries to begin speeding up the pace of talented women attaining clout title positions who have, to this point, been thwarted by glass ceilings.

In 1984 Representative Geraldine Ferraro (D-New York) became the first female vice-presidential nominee of a major Party. In 2008 Senator Hillary Rodham Clinton (D-New York) made an historic but unsuccessful run for the Democratic Party's nomination for president. On August 29, 2008, Governor Sarah Palin (R-Alaska) was selected by Senator John McCain (R-Arizona) as the Republican Party's vice-presidential nominee. In her speech that day, Governor Palin acknowledged two women who paved a path before her – Geraldine Ferraro and Hillary Rodham Clinton. Governor Palin not only referenced the place in history Representative Ferraro and Senator Clinton have but also acknowledged the important role Senator Clinton played in potentially breaking a particular glass ceiling:

> "It was rightly noted...that Hillary [Clinton] left 18 million cracks in the highest, hardest glass ceiling in America. But it turns out the women of America aren't finished yet and we can shatter that glass ceiling once and for all."

Despite her optimism, Governor Palin's bid for the vice-presidency was unsuccessful and Senator Clinton was not the Democratic Party's nominee for President. A closer look at the 2008 election shows that it was not a good election cycle for the advancement of women in elected positions. Consider the following from the Center for American Women and Politics at Rutgers University:

- Eight women are serving as governors in 2009; same as 2008.
- 24 percent of women serve in statewide elective office in 2009, down from 28 percent in 2000.
- The U.S. Senate has 17 female members. There are ten newly-elected female House members. The class of 2008 includes less than half the number of women who first won office in 1992 – the so-called "year of the woman."
- Including incumbents and newcomers, a record number of women are serving in Congress, but still only 17 percent of its members will be female.

Where do these numbers rank us? Marie Cocco says America is on the same level of representation women have achieved in sub-Saharan Africa, Latin America, and the Caribbean. A United Nations tracking group estimates that it will take women 40 years to reach parity with men. Will it take women in the United States as long to reach parity with men in politics as it does the developing world?

Though women have made gains in breaking through glass ceilings, there is still much work to be done to achieve full equality. Men need to recognize that women should be full partners in the public sky. Men's skies benefit from the excellent support women give them. It's our turn to support women in the private and public sectors. It is only when men and women alike make the commitment to recognize glass ceilings for what they truly are, their exact causes, and become advocates for the advancement of women executives will be when I can look at my step-daughter, nieces, and great-nieces and not have to wonder "what might have been."

"Mother always told me, 'If if matters ten years from now, get right up and do it. If it doesn't matter, don't worry about it.' The theory always helped when I was working two full-time jobs, one part-time job, and had six children at home...Material things don't count for much – it's the human element that rewards."

– Helen Shoars

Reflections Under Glass

"Why does a lack of women at the top matter? Because we intuitively know — and studies have demonstrated — that when there is a critical mass of women in key decision-making positions within companies or on boards, good things happen. It attracts other talented women to join. When there is a critical mass of women, their voices are heard and not ignored."

Susan Ness, former Federal Communications Commissioner

"Perhaps the next few years will bring society to a place where women are no longer regarded with suspicion; where they are given the chance to prove their competence, rather than having to fight the assumption that they were hired because EEOC laws required it. Perhaps some of the old myths about women's unreliability and inability to handle pressure will finally be put to rest, and women will no longer be perceived as 'too aggressive' if they express their desire for career advancement. Perhaps in the near future, women will no longer have to choose between marriage and career..."

Donna L. Halper, Author of *Invisible Stars: A Social History of Women in American Broadcasting*

Asst. Professor of Communication, Lesley University, Cambridge, Massachusetts

"I would say don't make it a women's issue because it is not. Now, are we different than men, yes we are, but at the end of the day our success is measured or should be measured exactly the same way. Now I would strongly suggest that women should never feel alone and to know that there are many terrific women in this industry to meet with, network with and learn from. Just reach out. You may be surprised to know how many new friends you have."

Erica Farber, former Radio & Records CEO/Publisher

"In order to reach career goals, you need to collaborate, listen, learn, apply, and communicate information well. Have the stamina and discipline to apply what you pickup along the way to the fundamentals of management and leadership. Start sentences with 'perhaps', I wonder if' 'do you think?', 'I need some input', 'I think I may have made a mistake', 'What do you think?', 'How might we'?"

Val Maki, Senior Vice-President, Radio Division/Emmis Communications

"Lead by example. Don't compromise. Be empathetic. Inspire people. Encourage a balanced life. Toot your own horn. Negotiate better. Encourage and mentor other women. Understand the business. Laugh often."

Joan Gerberding, Principal, NextGenMarketing

7 PUTTING IT ALL TOGETHER

You've read about the secret nature of glass ceilings and how to overcome those invisible barriers. Now it's time for you to apply what you've read in this book to you and your career path. This chapter will require you to examine your career, your industry, your life, and put together a plan for you to smash the barriers impeding your career progress.

To which executive position do you aspire?

_____

At what level is the glass ceiling in your industry?

_____

At what level is the glass ceiling in your company?

_____

What obstacles do you perceive stand in your way?

_____

What are some of the unwritten rules in your company?

_____

Which archetype do you see most in your workplace among
female executives…geisha, bitch, or guy?

_____

Who are influential women you know who could be group mentors?

_____

Who are or could be your internal champions?

_____

What networking opportunities are there in your industry? In
your company? In your community?

_____

What online networking websites would allow you to connect
with influential women in your industry?

_____

Who could you nominate to be on your Personal Board of
Directors?

Claifier: _____

Connector: _____

Challengers: _____

Sage: _____

Afterword

Women Under Glass is the first step toward, once and for all, breaking the artificial barriers holding women back. The next step is to chronicle stories of women from the frontlines who have broken or are trying to shatter glass ceilings. If you've encountered glass ceilings, I welcome your stories. Go to www.womenunderglass.com and click "Share A Glass Ceiling Story" and share your experiences. The best stories will be included in the next book. You can also check out my blog at womenunderglass.wordpress.com. Check out the Women Under Glass Facebook fan page.

Acknowledgements

To the Great I Am, thank you for loving me, for never giving up on me, for guiding me through the challenges of life, and for surrounding me with people who have been such a blessing.

Writing a book is a team effort and this book is no different. I would like to express my gratitude to Doctor George Ecker, Doctor Stephanie Fraser–Beekman, Doctor Carl Beekman, Doctor Kirstin Cronn-Mills, and Mrs. Lisa Miller for their counsel, advice, support, encouragement, and guidance throughout my research process.

A standing ovation and a grateful heart to Joan Gerberding, Erica Farber, Val Maki, and the members of Mentoring and Inspiring Women; and to the Mentoring and Inspiring Women protégées, whose candor in our conversations provided terrific insight. This work would not have been possible if not for the MIWs and their protégées.

Kudos to Eric Rhoads at Radio Ink, Paul McLane at Radio World, and Jim du Bois at the Minnesota Broadcasters Association for providing a forum for my ideas. Kudos also to Donna L. Halper and Nicki Gilmour for their support and being continuing advocates and champions for women everywhere.

A tip of the cap to Kevin Hogan whose expertise and encouragement helped to make this book a reality.

Thanks to my wife Julie, who is my heart of hearts and my biggest fan.

Sources

Agozino, B. (1995). Methodological issues in feminist research. *Quality & Quantity 29*, 287-298.

Axtell, R. E., Briggs, T. Corcoran, M. & Lamb, M. B. (1997). *Dos and taboos around the world for women in business* (1st ed.). New York, NY: John Wiley & Sons.

Barnier, L. A. (1982). A study of the mentoring relationships: An analysis of its relation to career and adult development in higher education and business. *Dissertation Abstracts International, 42(7-A),* 3012-3013.

Bernhard, L.A. (1984). Feminist research in nursing research Poster session presented at The First International Congress on Women's Health Issues, Halifax, Nova Scotia.

Boles, J. K., & Long-Hoeveler, D. (1996). *From the goddess to the glass ceiling: A dictionary of feminism* (1st ed.). Lanham, MD: Madison Books.

Bolton, E. (1980). A conceptual analysis of the mentor relationship in the career development of women. *Adult Education, 30,* 195-207.

Bruzzese, A. May 2, 2005, *Des Moines Register, 8C*

Butler, J. (1999). *Gender trouble* (2nd ed.). New York, NY: Routledge.

Business Week Online (2000, October 3). Q&A with American Bar Association President Martha Barnett. *BW Online*. Retrieved June 30, 2006, from www.businessweek.com/careers/content/oct2000/ca2000103_488.htm

Business Week (2001, April 30). *Wanted: More diverse directors.* Retrieved June 30, 2006, from www.businessweek.com/magazine/content/01_18/b3730116.htm

Butler, J. (1999). *Gender trouble* (2nd ed.). New York, NY: Routledge.

Cain, M. (1990). Realist philosophy and standpoint epistemologies of feminist criminology as a successor science. In L. Gelsthorpe and A. Morris (eds.), *Feminist Perspectives in Criminology*. Milton Keynes, Open University Press.

Cheng, B. (2006, June 14). *Gen X women: Moving up.* Retrieved on June 30, 2006, from www.businessweek.com/print/careers/content/jun2002/ca20020614_3443.htm

Clark, H. (2006, March 8). Are women happy under the glass ceiling? Retrieved on June 30, 2006, from www.forbes.com/2006/03/07/glass-ceiling-opportunities--cx_hc_0308glass_print.html

CNN   May 4, 2009 http://money.cnn.com/magazines/fortune/fortune500/2009/womenceos/

Cocco, M. (2008, November 20). *Real Clear Politics.* Retrieved December 13, 2008, from The Glass Ceiling Holds Strong: http://www.realclearpolitics.com/articles/2008/11/the_glass_ceiling_holds_strong.html

Estrich, S. (2000). *Sex and power.* New York, NY: Riverhead Books.

Evans, G. (2000). *Play like a man, win like a woman: What men know about success that women need to learn* (1st ed.). New York, NY: Broadway Books.

Evans, M. (1990). The problem of gender for women's studies. *Women's Studies International Forum, 13,* 457-462.

Falk, E. & Grizard, E. (2003). *The glass ceiling persists: The 3rd annual AAPC report on women leaders in communication companies.* The Annenberg Public Policy Center of the University of Pennsylvania.

Fine, M. G. (1995). *Building successful multicultural organizations: Challenges are opportunities.* Westport, CT: Quantum Books.

French, J. R., & Raven, B. H. (1959). The bases of social power. In D. Cartwright (Ed.), *Studies in social power.* Ann Arbor, MI: University of Michigan Press.

Gallagher, M. (2001, Winter). Reporting on gender in journalism: Why do so few women reach the top? *Nieman Reports, 55*(4), 63-65.

Gallos, J.V. (1989). Exploring women's development: Implications for career theory, practice, and research. In Arthur, M.B., Hall, D.T., & Lawrence, B.S. (Eds.) *Handbook of Career Theory*, Cambridge, MA: Cambridge University Press.

Gifford, D. (2001, July 9). Wise up, wall street radio companies. *Radio Ink, 16*(12), 16.

Greenberg, J. (2002, 3rd ed.). *Managing behavior in organizations.* Upper Saddle River, NJ: Prentice Hall.

Greenberg, J. (2002, 3rd ed.). *Managing behavior in organizations.* Upper Saddle River, NJ: Prentice Hall.

Halper, D. L. (2001). *Invisible stars: A social history of women in American broadcasting* (1st ed.). Armonk, NY: M.E. Sharpe.

Harding, S. (1986). *The science question in feminism.* Milton Keynes. Open University

Haring-Hildore, M. (1987, November). Mentoring as a career enhancement strategy for women. *Journal of Counseling & Development, 66*(3), 147-148.

Heffernan, M. (2002, August). The female CEO ca. 2002. *Fast Company, 61*, 58-66.

Heim, P. & Golant, S. K. (1995). *Shattering the glass ceiling* (1st ed.). New York, NY:Fireside.

Helgesen, S. (1995a). *The female advantage: Women's ways of knowing* (7th ed.). New York, NY: Doubleday.

Helgeson, S. (1995b). *The web of inclusion* (1st ed.). New York, NY: Doubleday.

Hooks, B. (2000). *Feminist theory: From margin to center* (2nd ed.). Cambridge, MA South End Press.

Hurley, Jennifer A.(2007) . "Introduction." Opposing Viewpoints: Feminism. Ed. Jennifer A. Hurley. San Diego: Greenhaven Press, 2000. August 2004. Accessed 27 January 2007. <http://www.enotes.com/feminism-article/41591>.

Ilgen, D. R., & Youtz, M. A. (1986). Factors affecting the evaluation and development of minorities in organizations. In K. M. Rowland, & G. R. Ferris (Eds.), *Research in personnel and human resource management* (Vol. 4, pp. 307-337). Greenwich, CT: JAI Press.

Keating, L. (2002, January/February). Women mentoring women: The rewards of giving. *Women in Business, 54*(1), 28.

Kram, K. E. (1985). *Mentoring at work: Developmental relationships in organizational life*. Glenview, IL: Scott-Foresman.

Kram, K. E. (1985b). Improving the mentoring process. *Training and Development Journal, 39*(4), 40-43.

Kram, K. E., & Isabella, L. A. (1985). Mentoring alternatives: The role of peer relationships in career development. *Academy of Management Journal, 28,* 110-132.

Kremer, B. (1993). Learning to say no: Keeping feminist research for ourselves. *Women's Studies International Forum, 13*, 463-467.

Leider, R. (2005). *Create a Personal Board of Directors*. Retrieved on May 7, 2005, from www.fastcompany.com/articles/2000/03/l0300a.html

Levinson, D. J., Darrow, C. N., Klein, E. B., Levinson, M.H., & McKee, B. (1978). *Seasons of a man's life*. Englewood Hills: Prentice-Hall.

Liff, S. & Ward, K. (2001, January). Distorted views through the glass ceiling: The construction of women's understandings of promotion and senior management positions. *Gender, Work, & Organization, 8*(1), 19-35.

Mattei, N. J. (2001, October). Mentoring. *Leadership and Management in Engineering, 1*(4), 41-47.

McGinn, D. (2006). Getting back on track. *Newsweek*, CXLVIII (13). September 25, 2006.

Mies, M. (1983). Towards a methodology for feminist research. In Bowles, G. & Klein, R.D. (Eds) *Theories of Women's Studies*. London: RKP.

Mount Holyoke College (1998, March 20). Top corporate players, all MHC alums, tell how they smashed the 'glass ceiling'. *College Street Journal*, 11(23). Retrieved on September 9, 2006, from www.mtholyoke.edu/offices/comm/csj/980320/2glass.html

Moss, L., Lawrence, L., Topham, L., Porter, R., & Smith, J. (2008, September 8). *Mail Online.* Retrieved December 13, 2008, from http://www.dailymail.co.uk/female\article-1052597

Nelson, D. L., & Quick, J. C. (1985). Professional women: Are distress and disease inevitable? *Academy of Management Review, 10,* 206-218.

Nelson, L. Shanahan, S. & Olivetti, J. (1997, August). Power, empowerment, and equality: Evidence for the motive of feminists, nonfeminists, and antifeminists. *Sex Roles, 37*(3-4), 227-249.

Noe, R. A. (1988, January). Women and mentoring: A review and research agenda. *Academy of Management Review, 13*(1), 65-78.

O'Donnell, L. (2009). Networking your way to the boardroom. Retrieved on October 19, 2009, from http://www.theglass-hammer.com/news/2009/10/13/networking-your-way-to-the-boardroom/#more-3206

Oliver, D. (2002, December 9). Taking aim at the glass ceiling. *Radio Ink,* 17(23), 74-76.

Newsweek (2006). *Leading the way.* Retrieved on September 21, 2006, from www.msnbc.com/id/14870541/site/newsweek

Newsweek (2006, September 25). Leading the Way. *Newsweek,* CXLVIII (13).

Parker, V.A. & Kram, K.E. (1993, March/April). Women mentoring women: Creating conditions for connection. Business Horizons, 36, (2), 42-52.

Parkin, F. (1994). Marxism and class theory: A bourgeois critique. In D.B. Grusky (Ed.), *Social stratification: Class, race, and gender in sociological perspective.* Boulder, CO: Westview Press

Parkin, F. (1994). Social stratification: Class, race, and gender in sociological perspective. In D. B. Grusky (Ed.), *Marxism and class theory: A bourgeois critique.* Boulder, CO: Westview Press

Patterson, V. (2006). Breaking the glass ceiling: What's holding women back? *Career Journal.com* Retrieved on August 22, 2006, from www.careerjournal.com

Rader, B. (2004). Mentors help break glass ceiling. From Cincinnati Business Courier, October 22, 2004. Accessed 1 Janauary 2007 from www.bizjournals.com/bizwomen/cincinnati/content/story.html?story_id=1012323

Radio Ink (2000, January 24). Heirs apparent. *Radio Ink, 15*(2), 30.

Radio Ink (2005b). *MIW report: Women manage 15% of radio stations.* Retrieved on March 30, 2005, from www.radioink.com/HeadlineEntry.asp?hid= 127972&pt=todaynews

Ridgeway, C. L. (2001). Gender, status, and leadership. *The Society for the Psychological Study for Social Issues, 57*(4), 637-655.

Ridgeway, C. L., & Smith-Louvin, L. (1999). The gender system and interaction. *Annual Review of Sociology, 25,* 191-216.

Riley, S. & Wrench, D. (1985). Mentoring among women lawyers. *Journal of Applied Social Psychology, 15,* 374-386.

Rothberg, D. (2006, June 8). *Tech's glass ceilings shows some cracks.* Retrieved on June 30, 2006, from www.eweek.com/print_article2/0,1217,a=1800457,00.asp

Ryan, E. (2001, February 5). He talks softly but carries a big axe. *Radio Ink, 16*(3), 20-22, 24-25.

Sachs, A. (1978). The myth of male protectiveness and the legal subordination of women. In C. Smart and B. Smart (eds.), *Women, Sexuality and Social Control.* London: Routledge & Kegan Paul.

Scott-Morgan, P. (1994). *The unwritten rules of the game: Master them, shatter them, and break through the barriers to organizational change.* New York, NY: McGraw-Hill, Inc.

Scraton, P. (1990). Scientific knowledge or masculine discourse? Challenging patriarchy in criminology. In L. Gelsthorpe and A. Morris (eds), *Feminist Perspectives in Criminology.* Milton Keynes, Open Unversity.

Shapiro, E. C., Haseltine, F. P., & Rowe, M. P. (1978). Moving up: Role models, mentors, and the "patron system." *Sloan Management Review, 19*(3), 51-58

Sharpe, R. (2000). As leaders, women rule. Retrieved on June 30, 2006, from www.businessweek.com/2000/00_47/b3708145.htm

Shoars, E. (2005). Women hold up half the sky: An examination of female-centered mentoring in the radio industry. *Dissertation.* Ann Arbor, MI: Pro Quest

Shoars, E. (2006). The bottomline to get women through radio's glass ceilings. *Radio Ink* 21 (11), 59.

Simpson, S. & Cacioppe, R. (2001). Unwritten ground rules: Transforming organization culture to achieve key business objectives and outstanding customer service. *Leadership & Organization Development, 22*(7/8), 394- 401.

Smart, C. (1990). Feminist approaches to criminology or post-modern woman meets atavistic man. In L. Gelsthorpe and A. Morris (eds), *Feminist Perspecitives in Criminology.* Milton Keynes, Open Unversity.

Smith, E. L., & Grenier, M. (1982). Sources of organizational power for overcoming structural obstacles. *Sex Roles, 8,* 733-746.

Stewart, L. P., & Gudykunst, W. B. (1982). Differential factors influencing the hierarchical level and number of promotions of males and females within an organization. *Academy of Management Journal, 25,* 586-597.

Sumner, C. (1990). Foucault, gender, and the censure of deviance. In L. Gelsthorpe and A. Morris (eds.), *Supra.*

Swoboda, M. J., & Millar, S. B. (1986). Networking-mentoring: Career strategy of women in academic administration. *Journal of NAWDAC, 49,* 8-13.

Taylor, S. (2009). Study: Women Create Their Own Glass Ceiling. http://hrguru.monster.com/news/articles/2855-study-women-create-their-own-glass-ceiling Retrieved on September 19, 2009.

Tischler, L. (2004, February). Where are the women? *Fast Company, 1*(79), 52-55, 58, 60.

Tomaskovic-Devey, D. (1993). *Gender and racial inequality at work: The sources and consequences of job segregation*. Ithaca, NY: ILR Press.

Valien, V. (1999). Why so slow? The advancement of women. Cambridge, MA: MIT Press.

Wall Street Journal (2006, June 22). Surveying the field: Cracking the glass ceiling. Retrieved on June 30, 2006, from www.careerjournal.com

Weber, M. (1978). *Economy and society: An outline of interpretive sociology*. Berkeley, CA: University of California Press.

Wiehl, L. (2007). The 51% minority. New York: Balantine

Wilkinson, S. (ed)(1986). *Feminist social psychology: Developing theory and practice*. Milton Keynes: Open University Press.